T0323902

Cambridge Elements ≡

Elements in Publishing and Book Culture
edited by
Samantha Rayner
University College London
Leah Tether
University of Bristol

LIBRARIES AND THE ACADEMIC BOOK

Matthew J. Shaw
The Queen's College, Oxford

CAMBRIDGE
UNIVERSITY PRESS

CAMBRIDGE
UNIVERSITY PRESS

Shaftesbury Road, Cambridge CB2 8EA, United Kingdom

One Liberty Plaza, 20th Floor, New York, NY 10006, USA

477 Williamstown Road, Port Melbourne, VIC 3207, Australia

314–321, 3rd Floor, Plot 3, Splendor Forum, Jasola District Centre,
New Delhi – 110025, India

103 Penang Road, #05–06/07, Visioncrest Commercial, Singapore 238467

Cambridge University Press is part of Cambridge University Press & Assessment,
a department of the University of Cambridge.

We share the University's mission to contribute to society through the pursuit of
education, learning and research at the highest international levels of excellence.

www.cambridge.org
Information on this title: www.cambridge.org/9781108729796

DOI: 10.1017/9781108688017

First published 2024

A catalogue record for this publication is available from the British Library.

ISBN 978-1-108-72979-6 Paperback
ISSN 2514-8524 (online)
ISSN 2514-8516 (print)

Libraries and the Academic Book

Elements in Publishing and Book Culture

DOI: 10.1017/9781108688017

First published online: December 2024

Matthew J. Shaw
The Queen's College, Oxford

Author for correspondence: Matthew J. Shaw, matthew.shaw@queens.ox.ac.uk

ABSTRACT: This Element explores the history of the relationship between libraries and the academic book. It provides an overview of the development of the publishing history of the scholarly – or academic – book, and related creation of the modern research library. It argues that libraries played an important role in the birth and growth of the academic book, and explores how publishers, readers and libraries helped to develop the format and scholarly and publishing environments that now underpin contemporary scholarly communications. It concludes with an appraisal of the current state of the field and how business, technology and policy are mapping a variety of potential routes to the future.

KEYWORDS: libraries, publishing, academic, book, communications

ISBNs: 9781108729796 (PB), 9781108688017 (OC)

ISSNs: 2514-8524 (online), 2514-8516 (print)

Contents

'Ah! you are a happy fellow,' said Mr. Farebrother, turning on his heel and beginning to fill his pipe. 'You don't know what it is to want spiritual tobacco–bad emendations of old texts, or small items about a variety of Aphis Brassicae, with the well-known signature of Philomicron, for the 'Twaddler's Magazine;' or a learned treatise on the entomology of the Pentateuch, including all the insects not mentioned, but probably met with by the Israelites in their passage through the desert; with a monograph on the Ant, as treated by Solomon, showing the harmony of the Book of Proverbs with the results of modern research. You don't mind my fumigating you?'

(George Eliot, *Middlemarch*, 1872)

Some observers believe that the new electronic technologies will have considerably more far-reaching effects, that their emergence signals the beginning of a fundamental shift in accepted practices governing the dissemination of ideas and even their development. According to that view, the institutions, practices, and forms of a print culture will undergo complete transformation or in some instances disappear altogether. The self-sufficient research library, the scholarly publisher, the printed book, the monograph, the learned journal, the process of peer review, and copyright practice – these and other familiar elements of the current system are all implicitly challenged by electronic technologies

(*University Libraries and Scholarly Communication: A Study Prepared for the Andrew W. Mellon Foundation* (The Association of Research Libraries, 1992), p. 4)

Introduction

In the early spring of 2020, the novel coronavirus upended everyday life. Libraries across the world shut their doors with no clear idea of when they would open again or in what circumstances. Compounded by the pandemic's wider uncertainty and fear, within academia, students, academics, and librarians keenly felt the loss of physical access to libraries, their collections, spaces and in-person services. While library staff and readers were denied access to their buildings – by law in the United Kingdom, except for the National Health Service and some other medical libraries – they were not *closed*. Library workers continued from home, and on site when permitted, supplying a range of services, from scanning on demand and 'virtual reading rooms' to 'click and collect' or 'kerbside pickup' in the USA. The Bodleian Libraries' motto of 'Keep Oxford Reading' could easily be adapted for academic (and public) libraries in villages, towns, and cities across the land.[1] While the pandemic offered a challenge to librarians' provision of spaces and works on paper, it shone a spotlight on the affordances and frictions of digital collections and remote services. e-Books, online databases, digitised historical texts, audiobooks, and digital mapping, all of which have increasingly been foregrounded in library collections (and acquisitions budgets) over the last two decades or longer, enabled the library to be offered remotely to wherever readers were in lockdown.

Such provision was, of course, subject to many constraints, from access to the internet to licencing restrictions. Many providers of digital resources extended what was on offer for free, in part out of a desire to help in the pandemic, and perhaps also with an eye to post-pandemic sales – after all, a crisis, as the economist Paul Romer once said, is a terrible thing to waste.[2] By

---

[1] C. Kamposiori, 'Virtual Reading Rooms and Virtual Teaching Spaces in Collection Holding Institutions. An RLUK Report on Current and Future Developments', RLUK, April 2022, retrieved 2 November 2023 from www.rluk.ac.uk/portfolio-items/virtual-reading-rooms-and-virtual-teaching-spaces-in-collection-holding-institutions.

[2] J. Rosenthal, 'On Language', *New York Times Magazine*, 31 July 2009, retrieved 31 October 2022 from www.nytimes.com/2009/08/02/magazine/02FOB-onlanguage-t.html.

no means universal, since many suppliers required an existing subscription or purchase of part of the package, it highlighted how much could be done digitally. Libraries' responses to the pandemic brought into heightened relief a series of developments, challenges, and opportunities that the profession has been grappling with since the 1990s: digitisation, licensing, the purpose of physical space, the visibility of libraries when acting as brokers to information, and divergence between scholarly publishing models for the arts, humanities, and the sciences.

The pandemic also affected publishers, sometimes in financially beneficial ways. Trade books showed a marked increase in sales, benefitting from lockdown habits and an infrastructure enabling easy shipping of books (predominantly by the US commercial behemoth Amazon). Consumer sales rose 9 per cent during 2019.[3] Academic publishing suffered in comparison. In the USA, for example, higher education spending collapsed, in part because of the temporary closure of many libraries and a response to budget concerns resulting from a change in admissions fees, state funding cuts, and a hit many endowments took from the (temporary) fall in the stock markets caused by the pandemic.[4] Many scholarly presses already producing open access works, combining free at point of use digital copies with print-on-demand books, found their business models well suited to the new, digital environment. The pandemic, set against a broader backdrop of shifts in higher education, brought to light many of the tensions inherent in what is termed 'scholarly communications', as libraries, publishers, funding bodies and higher education institutions rearrange long-established modes of acquisition, licencing and use of copyright. While academic libraries and books appear to be as inseparable, there are signs that this link is not as secure as it once was.

As such, it seems timely to explore these questions, and this present 'micrograph' examines the connection between libraries and the academic

---

[3] A. Flood, 'UK Book Sales Soared during the Pandemic', *Guardian*, 27 April 2021, retrieved 4 October 2022 from www.theguardian.com/books/2021/apr/27/uk-book-sales-soared-in-2020-despite-pandemic.

[4] C. Guren, T. McIlroy, and S. Sieck, 'COVID-19 and Book Publishing: Impacts and Insights for 2021', *Pub Res Q* 37 (1) 2021, 1–14.

book, offering an overview of their long-entwined history, the current complex library and monographic landscape, and some thoughts on potential direction of travel. *Libraries and the Academic Book* has been written in the UK and much of its focus is on the British higher education system and publishing networks, but includes Europe, America, and beyond where possible. The story it tells will, I hope, bridge what is often called the history of the book with library science and history, and help to show that the history of the academic book cannot be told without the important contribution of libraries; and that although the academic book's future is still tied to that of the library, the ties might be fraying if care is not given to them.

1 The Academic Book

In *Portable Magic*, her 2022 study of books as things in the world, Emma Smith observes that the question 'What is a book?' usually prompts answers that are 'either reasonably uncontentious or insufferably pretentious'.[5] Smith also draws attention to the many exceptions that make any definition fallible. For example, in 1964, UNESCO defined a book as a 'non-periodical publication of at least forty-nine pages, exclusive of the cover pages, published in the country and made available to the public'. Smith notes that this definition that identified books as 'commercially produced codices' excluded 'many children's picture books, self-published works, and imposed an arbitrary length'; Charles Dickens' novels, first published in serial form, would fall foul of UNESCO's description. An acquisitions librarian might also wonder about the implications for 'monographs-in-series' (the term used for a group of scholarly or scientific books published sequentially), but since these books rarely appear on a set schedule, they fall outside of the definition of 'periodical'. Inclusion of what constitutes a 'book' in libraries beyond the West, where, for example, writing stored on ostraca, papyrus rolls or the hide and bark codices of Mesoamerica, might also fruitfully enrich any definition.

For most people, of course, the question doesn't much matter, expect perhaps when wondering whether to purchase the book (in hardback or paperback), as Kindle electronic licence, or as an Audible book. But for librarians, with their concern for organising and making information available, the question is perhaps more critical, and the answer might also have financial and budgetary implications. Up until 1 March 2020, for example, eBooks were VAT-rated in the UK at 20 per cent, unlike printed books which have long been considered essential items, and so exempt from this tax. As part of its Covid-19 response, the government brought planned legislation forward 7 months, arguing for the need to make 'reading more accessible as people stay at home'.[6] Audiobooks, however, continue to be taxed.

---

[5] E. Smith, *Portable Magic: A History of Books and Their Readers* (Allen Lane, 2022), p. 276.

[6] 'VAT scrapped on E-publications', gov.uk, retrieved 31 October 2022 from www .gov.uk/government/news/vat-scrapped-on-e-publications.

Defining 'What is an academic book?' might be especially tricky, and deals with a moving target.[7] Pulp fiction or trade books might often be the subject of humanities or social science research, for example, while the speedy developments in certain fields, such as computer science, might quickly transform the most current of monographs into historical relics. Academic, perhaps, but not serving the same purpose as an up-to-date work. An academic or scholarly book might prove to be difficult to define, as it risks becoming all-encompassing.

Bibliographically, the question 'What is a book' throws up a set of increasingly complex answers, many of which revolve around matters of issue or edition, making it more of a question of 'which book is this?'. Extensive principles of bibliographic description have been developed to be able to identify and chart the printing of books from the hand-press era to that of modern publishing. Book collectors also favour the first edition, and especially the 'first state' – the initial book as it first appeared from the printers, before the presses were set up to produce a new impression. Before this, of course, lie printers' proofs, authors and publishers' drafts, and review copies. All of these are means of conveying the intellectual and artistic work of its author or creator. The work of cataloguing books revolves around this dichotomy, that is between a physical book and its intellectual work. Library cataloguers – or at least those working within the current Resource Description and Access standard – now think in terms of works, expressions, manifestations, and item. In this important international standard, the 'work' is the immaterial intellectual product, such as the story of Dr Frankenstein's monster. The 'expression' is its physical manifestation, such as a published novel; another expression might be the work translated into French or Russian. A 'manifestation' would be, for example, the first edition or a recent reprint, while the 'item' is the individual book, with its own annotations, binding, and printing errors, on the library shelf, or possibly a Uniform Resource Locater that provides a digital version of the

---

[7] 'What Is an Academic Book?', *The Academic Book of the Future*, retrieved 31 October from academicbookfuture.org/2015/04/17/what-is-an-academic-book. Cf. J. J. Regazzi, *Scholarly Communications: A History from Content as King to Content as Kingmaker* (Rowman & Littlefield, 2015), p. 47.

Mary Shelley's tale. The things described at various points along this hierarchy might, to a greater or lesser extent, be thought of as a 'book'. Aware of some of the potential complexities, it seems sensible to turn from this broad question – perhaps leaving it to book artists, such as Ben Denzer's *20 Slices* (2018) – a book constructed from American cheese, to explore the boundaries of the codex – and turn to the academic book.

1.1 The Learned Book

What we now consider to be the 'academic book' has a long history; indeed, the many of the earliest printed books created might be considered to be 'academic'. Returning to these origins help to reveal how the book has developed, but also help to lay bare the practicalities around the making, selling and reading of books, the structures of which retain many of the same characteristics. As Roderick Conway Morris suggests in a review of an exhibition on the printer and publisher Aldus Manutius (1449–1515) – whose Aldine press caused him to 'became so famous that among educated Europeans it was sufficient to refer to him by his Christian name' – almost everything that was going to happen in book publishing – from pocket books, instant books and pirated books, to the concept of author's copyright, company mergers, and remainders – occurred during the early days of printing, the subsequent centuries offering but variations on a theme.'[8]

Early modern European scholarship was not distinct from the marketplace. What might be termed the 'learned book' – the antecedent of the modern 'academic book' – also turned intellectual labour and knowledge into a potentially sellable commodity. Following the innovations in European moveable type in the late fifteenth century, and the discovery of a market for the printed text alongside scribal production, printers and booksellers developed a sophisticated market, reliant on a network of authors and consumers, middlemen and drawing on both capital and credit. Specialised printer/publishers, such as Johann Froben in Basel, and

---

[8]   R. C. Morris, 'The Great Publisher', review of 'Aldo Manuzio e l'Ambiente Veneziano (1495–1515)', Liberia Sansonviniana, Venice, *Times Literary Supplement*, 23 September 1994, p. 20, quoted in I. Maclean, *Scholarship, Commerce, Religion: The Learned Book in the Age of Confessions, 1560–1630* (Harvard University Press, 2012), p. 2.

international fairs, notably the Frankfurt-am-Main fair, as well as those in Paris, Lyon, Vienna or Nuremberg, underpinned scholarly communication at this time – largely conducted in the transnational language of Latin.[9] The printing press did not replace scribal production; and as historians of the book are keen to stress, the two coexisted for centuries. But the new technology did 'upset the traditional rhythms of trade in the book world'.[10] While most manuscripts were commissioned by a patron, in a relatively direct relationship with the scribe, printers instead had to gauge a market that probably extended across Europe. Financial calculations, the investment of capital, the management of stock, and relationships with other booksellers could make or break the fortunes of a printer. The varied demand of the marketplace continued to play an important role in the history of print – something that modern publishers (and indeed libraries) are well aware.

While the focus of early printers may have been on what might today be termed academic works, aimed at scholars and learned readers, with editions of classical texts, works of the church Fathers and later commentators, printers discovered that there were also other potentially profitably markets which sought out books of a less 'academic' nature. Aldus sought a broader market beyond works that fuelled 'the arcane disputes of pettifogging pedants and schoolmen', creating texts for 'cultured men and women of his age'.[11] To aid this expansion, Aldus' innovations included an 'italic' typeface, which could be more easily read and allowed more words to be fitted happily on a page, and pocketable 'octavo' format for his editions of Greek and Latin, and, increasingly, Italian texts. The distinction between 'trade' books – better selling, distributed through resellers, and aimed a wider audience and 'academic' books was clearly apparent in this era; although of course, much as today, there were also large areas of overlap. Printer's profits, such as they were, came from elsewhere, from the staples that developed from the 1450s: as the book historians James Raven and Joran Proot list, 'Bibles, prayer books,

---

[9] Maclean, *Scholarship, Commerce, Religion.*

[10] A. Pettegree and A. der Weduwen, *The Library: A Fragile History* (Profile Books, 2021), p. 77.

[11] Morris, 'The Great Publisher'.

psalters, almanacs, religious and instructional primers, chapbooks, ballads and prognostications'.[12] To this we might add, as society became more literature, the jobbing work of most printers, such as posters, official publications or records, indentures, forms, calling cards, and so forth.

The history of the book – and the academic book is not different – is in part a numbers game. We do not really know how many books were published in the past. Many more do not survive, it is thought, than do. 'Ghost books', recorded in sales catalogues and endpapers, give a sense of a far greater number of publications than survive in our libraries. Many of these are likely to be more ephemeral items than learned or academic books, but there will still be some. The mathematical modelling of manuscript production – and loss – recently undertaken by a team in Oxford and the Netherlands, suggests over 60 per cent of English manuscripts have not survived, pointing to a loss of the medieval academic record.[13] Might the same statistical methods give a sense of early modern printing landscape, or confirm our existing assumptions and best guesses? Certainly, the eighteenth century saw a rapid increase in the number of publications. To take two markers suggested by Jeffrey Freeman, the number of book titles listed in the Leipzig fair rose from 1,360 titles in 1763 to 6,801 in 1793, while the numbers recorded in the English Short Title Catalogue (another important academic bibliographic tool created by the collaboration of teams across libraries) for that span of time are 2,701 and 6,801.[14] Many of these books, it should be noted, were published in the national languages, rather than Latin, marking a definitive shift away from the transnational language of scholarship.[15]

---

[12] J. Raven and G. Proot, 'Renaissance and Reformation', in J. Raven (ed.), *Oxford Illustrated History of the Book* (Oxford University Press, 2020), p. 162.

[13] M. Kestemont, F. Karsdorp, E. de Bruijn, et al., 'Forgotten Books: The Application of Unseen Species Models to the Survival of Culture', *Science* 375 (6582) 2022, pp. 765–769.

[14] Such modern collaboration has echoes of earlier cooperation between libraries in medieval and early modern cultures, notably in the sharing of lists of books or other forms of catalogues.

[15] J. Freedman, 'Enlightenment and Revolution', in Raven (ed.), *Oxford Illustrated History* (Oxford University Press), p. 226.

The market for such learned books consisted of monasteries and individuals with their personal libraries rather than university libraries. It continued to be a market that expanded, fuelled by the growth in the merchant and professional classes, who required works of reference or training in their respective trades or professions, be they bookkeeping, navigation or the law. For example, one study of 340 doctors and lawyers in the seventeenth-century Dutch Republic reveals that the average size of their collections was around 1,000 books.[16] Printers keenly developed texts for these markets.

Such publishing always took place within a broader social and cultural context, which not only authorised what could be printed – through state censorship and the granting of licences – but helped to grant credibility and authority to what was printed. Such gatekeeping or use of prestige came not from the universities as the scholarly societies and informal connections between humanist writers and thinkers. From the sixteenth century, the new approaches towards investigating the natural world and the founding of organisations such as the Royal Society in London, helped to found the structures of scientific printing. From the beginning, the importance of correspondence, collaboration (and refutation) shaped the contours of scientific printing, giving special importance to the journal format, which allowed for shorter pieces, quick publication, wide dissemination, and speedier responses. Groups such as the Royal Society became publishers themselves, and their members helped to fund the works such as the Society's first book, Robert Hooke's *Micrographia* (1665) or Isaac Newton's *Principia* (1687). Such texts required specialised printing techniques, notably the use of woodcuts within the text to allow Newton's charts to be included alongside the relevant text, and detailed engravings produced by Hooke in his exploration of the miniature world revealed by the microscope. *Philosophical Transactions of the Royal Society* continues to be published today.

Such publications embody certain characteristics still common to the academic publications: the need to communicate complex ideas through specialised typography or illustration, to communicate to a particular community, and to be in explicit dialogue with them, whether through scholarly

---

[16] Pettegree and Weduwen, *The Library*, p. 128.

apparatus such as foot or side notes, or through providing a means of response in a journal. They also required accuracy and made use of several methods to assert their authority. Increased precision came from the use of correctors and other printshop practices, and from experiments such as peer review, such as that as undertaken by the Royal Society of Edinburgh in 1731. Book reviews, which offered a form of post-publication peer review originated in bibliographical works such as Conrad Gessner's magisterial *Bibliotheca universalis* (1545). Here Gessner included books that might considered 'bad', along with a short summary of the contents. Future bibliographers selected what they considered to be the 'best' books.[17] Booksellers' catalogues offered another form of judgement, including details of previous ownership, suggesting that some of the cachet of, for an example, an earlier duke's ownership might transfer with a successful bid for the item at the book fair auction.[18] German universities began to publish book reviews in journals from the late seventeenth century. The *Journal des sçavans* and the *Philosophical Transactions* of the Royal included book reviews along with the accounts of observations, experiments and reflections on natural philosophy. And in 1684, Pierre Bayle founded the *Nouvelles de la République des Lettres*, consisting entirely of book reviews. (It ended in 1687.) Such reviews included a useful summary (and thereby provided a form of translation if the work was in another language). For many, the historian of information Ann Blair suggests, books reviews 'stood in for reading the book itself'; a practice many may recognise today.[19]

By the nineteenth century, publishing houses had been firmly established as the dominant force in the printing landscape, largely replacing the more ad-hoc arrangements of the hand-press era, and working closely with scholarly societies to publish authoritative works. Still mainly family firms, shops such as Didot in France or F. A. Brockhaus in Germany, were able to outcompete smaller printers, who could not afford the invest-ment in new machinery, buildings and staff. Booksellers developed

[17] Ann Blair, 'Managing Information', in Raven (ed.), *Oxford Illustrated History* (Oxford University Press), p. 189.
[18] Blair, 'Managing Information', p. 188. [19] Blair, 'Managing Information', p. 192.

sophisticated systems of supply and stock management. They and publishers offered a range of careers, from editing to a host of production positions, from printing to binding. In some countries, publishers with an interest in the academic markets remained unconnected with universities, such as presses in the Low Countries or Germany. In the United Kingdom, the connection was likely to be closer, not least because since the sixteenth century, the universities of Oxford and Cambridge, along with City of London, were granted the royal privilege to print and which developed important university presses. While other English presses were granted such privileges from the seventeenth century, Oxford and Cambridge retained certain rights, such as that of printing almanacs and the Bible. In the nineteenth century, profits from printing the King James Bible were such that it enabled Oxford to build the University Museum. These financial underpinnings at both universities, augmented and by textbooks, school materials and trade publications such as dictionaries – both of which had near-exclusive markets in the British empire, enabled the publication of an extensive academic list (and from the last quarter of the twentieth century, journal subscriptions also became a valuable source of profit). University presses in the United States were more of a twentieth-century phenomenon, coexisting alongside commercial academic publishers and trade publishers with an interest in the scholarly market, such as W.W. Norton & Company.

This long history has created a rich ecosystem of academic publishing. Within this, a large number of types of books have been established, rather like the numerous exotic fauna observable in Australasia. What might a taxonomy look like? The central text (at least for the humanities) might be the academic *monograph*: in the historian Geoffrey Crossick's phrase, the 'cornerstone of academic writing', especially in the humanities. Offering a sustained examination of a topic in at least 80,000 words, and possibly much more, running over two or more volumes, the work's scope not only allows ideas and arguments to be given full consideration, but also the inclusion of important scholarly apparatus, such as footnotes, supporting materials in appendixes, bibliographies, and various indexes, such as place, subject, name, or general. It is the sort of work on which the Revd. Casaubon's labours in George Eliot's *Middlemarch* (and often perhaps equally confounding to those outside the academy). The formal expectations of the components that constitute a monograph have developed over time. For example, bibliographies only tended to be included from the early twentieth century, along with information about sources, while digital printing means that errata pages are now less common, as mistakes can be more easily corrected at a late stage of production if they are spotted, since books are rarely set in type. Different disciplines also have distinct styles of writing and expectations of format.

As a publication, academic books are more than monographs, and encompass the edited volume, the critical edition and facsimiles with contextual materials such as introductions. Conference proceedings, edited collections, museum and art gallery catalogues and specialist reference materials, such as specialised dictionaries all include vital material for academic work and typically include introductions or other commentaries that both aid understanding and are a contribution to knowledge in themselves. Such forms are not fixed, and there continues to be experiment what an academic book might be – the present Element is just one such example, being a series of shorter-form writing, a format that has expanded dramatically over the last decade. In 2021, in the United Kingdom, the Research Excellence Framework's (REF) assessment of what it terms Higher Education 'outputs' stressed the range of materials which could be assessed, such as translation, as well as performances and exhibitions. Many of these will be stored by a library, typically in digital form. Here we also see another aspect of the academic book – its potential as a site of experiment, but also closely linked to academic's career, reputation and the funding of their discipline and departments.[20] Contrary to the assumptions about hierarchies of publishers' imprimatur and the prestige of certain journals or monographs in series, the REF has consistently stressed that these aspects are not assessed, only the significance, rigour and originality of the work. In this context, the funding landscape also puts far more stress, and increasingly strictures, on open access publishing. Access to research outputs, rather than association with certain presses or publications is what is valued here. Definitions of what a book is, and what is valued (or disagreeable) about it, are thus important not just for this Element, but also contribute to how academia is shaped, or at least the flow of

[20] A. Csiszar, 'The Catalogue that Made Metrics, and Changed Science', *Nature*, 551 2017, pp. 163–165.

resources. These definitions certainly shape library collections, offering a means to somewhat automating what is purchased for a library, notably in what librarians terms a 'conspectus' approach to collecting. In this widespread methodology, monographs may fall inside (or outside) the library's collection development conspectus, while edited editions might be treated very differently.[21] Now that the contours of the academic book have been defined, it might be as well to turn to their relationship with the library.

---

[21] International Federation of Library Associations and Institutions (IFLA), *Guidelines for a Collection Development Policy Using the Conspectus Model*, retrieved 14 November 2022 from repository.ifla.org/handle/123456789/52.

2 Libraries

Is it easier to define a library than a book? There are certainly a wide range of types of libraries with a host of similarities and differences, from lively public libraries to august national institutions. Some are focussed on a wide audience, free to enter and borrow, with a host of public programmes, while others are private, and concentrate resolutely on serving particular professional needs, such as law libraries. Medical libraries in hospitals or other medical institutions fulfil a range of distinct and important needs. There are prison libraries, mobile libraries, cruise-ship libraries, museum libraries, society libraries. There are libraries with no physical books, but which provide access to large digital collections, while other libraries are forming sophisticated collaborative networks to reduce duplication and share resources, creating a library greater than the sum of its parts.[22] And there remain numerous private libraries, whether those belonging to wealthy individuals, to the library's members, such as The London Library or the Library Company in Philadelphia, or belonging to historic sites such as the large number of country house and other libraries under the custodianship of the National Trust in England, Wales and Northern Ireland. These libraries, of course, may also have a rich programme of outreach, access and engagement. But many libraries are naturally associated with an educational establishment as their primary mission, whether a school, college, university, or other institute of higher education. It is here that we find the academic book has a special importance.

All these types of libraries are united by a common function. They are places that have collected, and may continue to collect, books and, it should be stressed, other resources in a variety of formats, from manga to DIY tools. While libraries did not begin with the book – that is, the codex form of rectangular pages bound together sequentially between boards – but with the scroll, such as in the famous Library of Alexandria, books soon came to dominate them, beginning in the West with the Roman libraries, where the

---

[22] 'UK Distributed Print Book Collection (UKDPBC)', RLUK, retrieved 10 November 2023 from www.rluk.ac.uk/uk-distributed-print-book-collec tion-ukdpbc.

codex was found to be a more convenient means of storing writing from the first century CE (the so-called Nag Hammadi library in Egypt, for example, comprises of thirteen leather-bound papyrus codices).[23] While they are places where books are to be found, they are not simply warehouses or stores (although it might be noted that warehouses are also complicated places). Libraries are the result of imposition of an intellectual viewpoint of some kind by librarians, imposing a form of order – even if it is only date of accession or size – on their collection, whether through the library's physical organisation or in combination with catalogues of various kinds. Such views, often informed by the assumptions of academic disciplines, bring their own ontologies and hierarchies, risking erasures or caesuras identified in decolonial critiques of European and North American libraries. The collections also have some purpose to them, whether partly reflecting the acquisitive instincts of its owner in the case of the libraries of the great collectors such as J. Pierpoint Morgan's library in New York, or more generally today, as one definition of American libraries defines it, as 'the mission of educating, informing or entertaining a variety of audiences'.[24] More nobly, the library's purpose is to serve, and help to improve, society. A library is by this definition a collection of materials, and a site whose purpose is to connect with and serve a group or groups of people. Increasingly, the latter function – that of offering services and helping particular groups – may be seen to be the main purpose of the library.

The library has always possessed a close link between its collections, its built environment, and its users. Some of the first western libraries, for example, can be found among the churches of the earliest Christian believers. The Apostle Paul asked Timothy to 'bring the books' which he had left at Troas, pointing to small travelling book collections for these itinerant believers.[25] The earliest Christian monasteries in Egypt placed the copying

---

[23] E. Robson, 'The Ancient World', in Raven (ed.), *Oxford Illustrated History* (Oxford University Press), p. 44.

[24] G. M. Eberhart, *The Librarian's Book of Lists: A Librarian's Guide to Helping Job Seekers* (American Library Association, 2010).

[25] Pettegree and Weduwen, *The Library*, p. 32.

of texts at the heart of the prayerful life, and texts continued to be central to the monasteries that developed across Europe. In these, scriptoria contained the necessary labour and expertise to copy and produce manuscript books. Several million such texts, of which perhaps 90 per cent are now lost, were spread across Europe in these monastic libraries: an astonishing achievement and use of resources and time.[26] Many such libraries were in some ways practical. Concepts of teaching, Barbara Crosini suggests, 'placed the book as a repository of received knowledge at the centre of Christian culture', giving the library an important practical and spiritual role.[27]

2.1 Library Becomes the Tool to Access, and Manage Books
Answering the need for religious, and increasingly legal training, a new form of educational institution war born in Spain, Italy, Paris, and England: the university. In Oxford and elsewhere colleges and other places of residential learning began to accumulate collections of manuscripts. These became libraries, and wherever there were students, stationers set out their stall, selling writing materials and, in Italy, *pecaria*, copies of sections of key texts which were loaned and then returned, a kind of proto-circulating library. As the historian and palaeographer David Rundle notes, 'the presence of a university became a stimulus to the local book trade so that, for example, in the ramshackle space of Oxford's Catte Street, artisans gathered to transcribe, illuminate, and bind manuscripts, or sell them second hand'.[28] Higher education and the book trade, particularly the academic book, are old bedfellows indeed.

Within monasteries, books might be found in a cupboard in the cloister (an aumbry, from the Latin *armarium*) or in a book chest. From the late-medieval period, books were chained to desks, in order to make them accessible but also to protect them from removal, in a dedicated room known as a library. The first two libraries in renaissance Italy, that of the

[26] Kestemont, 'Forgotten Books'.

[27] B. Crosini, 'Byzantium', in Raven (ed.), *Oxford Illustrated History* (Oxford University Press), p. 78.

[28] D. Rundle, 'Medieval Western Europe', in Raven (ed.), *Oxford Illustrated History* (Oxford University Press), p. 130.

Dominicans of San Marco in Florence (1436–1443) and the Biblioteca
Malatestiana in Cesena's Franciscan convent. At the same time, the use of
books affected their physical shape. The Franciscan innovation of clerical
mobility created a need for religious texts that could be carried. Thinner
vellum meant width and weight could be reduced, and illuminated initials
replaced whole-page illuminations. Form followed function even in
beautiful illuminated manuscripts, such as the Macclesfield Psalter, that
today's readers are lucky to inherit, and often have access to online.

   The development of printing changed the nature of libraries. Manuscripts
remained important, not least as a symbol of the owner's status, but over time,
the speed and costs of printing, together with crucial changes in distribution
capacity, technological and economic developments such as paper production,
and printers', such as Aldus's, expansion into more secular markets.
Institutional libraries remained out of bounds for most, and only in the
seventeenth century did they potentially offer access for a largely male
group of clerics, the intelligentsia or nobility.[29] As the provision of print
expanded, and libraries did not just remain the province of ecclesiastical
institutions or princes, but could be found by the late-fifteenth century in the
homes of merchants, lawyers and others. As the historian Ann Blair reflects,
'forming a significant library became … a widely shared goal among the
elites.'[30] By the 1620s, the librarian Gabriel Naudé was persuaded to publish his
Advice on Establishing a Library, the first work on librarianship, 'concerning',
Naudé wrote, 'the choice of books, the means of procuring them, and the
arranging of them in the most useful and attractive manner for a handsome and
stately library.'[31] The work, which was translated into English by John Evelyn
in 1666, demonstrates the growing interest and financial investment in libraries
over this period. As Blair observes, while the library of a French magistrate
might consist of six dozen books in the late-fifteenth century, it might, as in the
case of Michel de Montaigne – another French magistrate – contain some

[29] J. Raven and D. Rundle, 'Renaissance and Reformation', in Raven (ed.), *Oxford
   Illustrated History* (Oxford University Press), p. 162.

[30] Blair, 'Managing Information', p. 185.

[31] G. Naudé, *Advice on Establishing a Library* (University of California Press, 1950), p. 9.

3,000 volumes, while a bibliophile duke might amass a collection of 30,000 volumes.[32]

The accumulation of such personal cultural capital could also lead to public benefit. Several of the great Western libraries of the period began to open their collections to scholars more broadly: such as the Bodleian Library, Oxford since 1602, the Mazarine Library in Paris since 1643. The Biblioteca Angelica opened its doors even wider in 1609, and as such is considered the oldest public library in Europe. As Naudé noted about the Ambrosian Library of Milan (in Eveyln's translation), 'is it not a thing altogether extraordinary, that any one may come into it, almost at all hours he will, stay as long as he pleases, see, read, extract what Authors he desires, have all the means and conveniences to do it, be it in publique or particular, and that without any other labour, than visiting it himself at the ordinary dayes, and hours, placing himself in the seats destin'd for this purpose'[33]

As Blair also notes, 'awareness of overabundance prompted the development of new genres – catalogues and other guides – . . . helped readers know about, select, obtain copies of books that matched their interests.'[34] Similarly, libraries assisted scholars in their labours. Libraries were more than increasingly complex, expensive (and beautiful) versions of aumbries. They added value to the collection of books, selecting, maintaining, and providing connections. While books in the West developed numerous systems of scholarly apparatus, or paratextual technical features that allowed easier of more scholarly use – such as tables of contents, the index, citations, glossaries, and so on – libraries also provided much of the scholarly infrastructure to provide a framework for the navigation and use of information. The number of printed books in the great collector Sir Robert Cotton's library is unknown, but probably ran to several thousand, with a large number of manuscripts. Some of the catalogues of his that are known to us handily arrange the contents into subject, classifications: 'Religio', 'Historia Ecclesiastica', 'Politicae', 'Ethicae', 'Astronomia',

---

[32] Blair, 'Managing Information', p. 185.

[33] G. Naudé, *Instructions Concerning Erecting of a Library* (University of California Press, 1950), pp. 88–89.

[34] Blair, 'Managing Information', p. 185.

'Cronologiae', 'Italia', 'Germanie scriptores', 'Turcay scriptores', 'Hungaria', 'Tartaria', 'Militare', 'Antiquitates', 'Epistolae', and 'De Artitectura' [sic]. More famously, Cotton's library is renowned for its physical arrangement, with busts of Roman emperors at the end of each bay, giving the volumes their distinctive titles: such as Vitellius A.x (*Beowulf*). Cotton's 'printed bookes', it seems, were kept in the upper study at Cotton House, Westminster in 'i iron prese & ix presses'.[35] Almost half a millennia after both Naudé and Cotton, proximity in subject matter remains a powerful tool in today's libraries for search and discovery, with many readers still believing in the importance of browsing and the hope of serendipitous discovery. Online systems continue to be developed that attempt to replicate the power of location in the ordering and uncovering of information. Algorithms, pioneered by search giants such as Alphabet (Google and YouTube), Meta (Facebook), and ByteDance (TikTok), might be considered the digital equivalent, in terms of the dominance, if not perhaps in comparable success. Library catalogues and online commercial services such as Academia. edu also make use of recommendations in this way.[36]

2.2 Catalogues

Following the thoughts of Naudé's advice, the Bodleian Library's third printed catalogue (1674) noted, that the reader could 'compile and index of books . . . which will aid him in personal study'. Institutions similarly drew on their colleagues' work: an interleaved copy of the Oxford catalogue formed the basis for the catalogue of the Mazarine Library in Paris. It might be as well to note here that international cataloguing collaboration and innovation continues – libraries regularly download, build upon and share their digital cataloguing records through a number of standardised processes, and are repurposed by internet search engines or expanded in union catalogues, such as WorldCat. Such digital transformation in many ways

---

[35] C. G. C. Tite, 'A Catalogue of Sir Robert Cotton's Printed Books?', *The British Library Journal* 17 (1) 1991, pp. 1–11.

[36] On the limits of shelf browsing, see D. Broadbent, 'The Highs and Lows of Physical Browsing: How Shelf Position Affects Book Usage in Academic Libraries', *The Journal of Academic Librarianship* 46 (1) 2020, 102074.

have opened up catalogues and provided the opportunity for interrogation in new ways, such as data analytics (and at the same time appear to decentre the catalogue in many people's experience of using a library). Catalogues borrowed from the innovations in booksellers' lists, prepared for the great bookselling fairs in Frankfurt, Paris and elsewhere, and transposed these marketing features into scholarly tools. In contrast to earlier manuscript catalogues, which simply listed materials in date of accession, and rarely offered a more helpful route way into the collections, such as alphabetisation, as was the case in the library at Dover Priory. Catalogues of printed libraries might be listed by author, by title, by topic, or also by size or date of acquisition, as this may have been linked to how the volumes were stored on the shelves. This may have been a product of the flexibility of moveable type (if the catalogue was printed, rather than in manuscript form), the production and availability of paper, the humanistic scholarly skills of the workforce, and also a result of the expanded nature of early modern libraries with their large and increasingly varied collections. Increased use and changes in the type of study may also have prompted the changes, too. Finally, for those responsible for the library, a proper catalogue helped with the day-to-day running of a library – checking that books were in their place, ensuring that duplicates were not acquired, and helping with donations or exchanges with other libraries.

The running of a library did indeed become a profession, or at least a defined part of a cleric or academic's role. Here, Naudé's advice was relatively simple: collect books in quantity, ensure that they are easily found and classified on the basis of their content, and for there to be usable catalogues. He also offered further advice on useful items to be kept in the library to assist in reading: clocks, globes, penknives for uncut pages, sand for blotting, ink, almanacs – and balls of jasper, commonly associated with scribes and scholars at this time. Yet once college or university libraries were fitted out with the necessary scholarly accruements (Naudé argued that decoration should not be too ornate) and had an established collection, their future growth was highly dependent on gifts. Few institutions had the funds or the inclination to acquire books on a regular basis. In the case of Oxford and Cambridge colleges, the collections would grow organically as expiring fellows might donate their libraries. Students might also be expected to purchase or donate titles for the collection as part of their fees, and a tradition of donation by old members also created important collections. However, many libraries also withered as the years passed. Books departed, perhaps never to return, with their readers. The usual perils of fire, flood and pests took their inevitable portion from the academy' stock of books.

2.3 Public Libraries

As reading as an activity expanded during the eighteenth century, the cost of purchasing books and the serial nature of reading helped to give rise to the commercial and public library in the West. From the eighteenth century, an increasing number of commercial libraries were established in towns and cities across Europe – such as *cabinets de lecture* in France – and the Americas. Numerous national libraries were also established, although typically were fairly restrictive in terms of who had access to their collections; however, scholars, intellectuals and academics were normally allowed. During the second half of the nineteenth century, the public library movement created the first libraries that were genuinely free and open to a wider public. In Britain the Public Libraries Act (1850) gave local authorities the power to establish a library in their town or borough; by 1914, over 5,000 library authorities oversaw the annual circulation of over 30 million volumes among an eager reading public. By 1903, the United States had more than 4,500 public libraries, containing some 55 million volumes. Such expansion in the reading material of the masses did not escape a number of moral panics – or at least bourgeois handwringing in the press – about what was being read. While there were fears that 'yellow fiction' or tales of gore offered an irresistible attraction to the burgeoning working classes, and which might pose a particular threat to the young or to women, popular tastes were more conservative and high-minded, showing the taste for Oliver Goldsmith or Walter Scott over gore in the bookstalls of nineteenth-century London.[37] Libraries also exercised their own gatekeeping, with library committees exercising stern moral judgement on what types of material might be selected for public stock.

---

[37] J. Rose, 'A Conservative Cultural Canon: Cultural Lag in British Working-Class Reading Habits', *Libraries & Culture*, 33 (1) 1998, pp. 98–104.

The demand for reading material reflected the explosion of print within wider society. Increasingly literacy and a range of new jobs in the industrialised West placed print at the centre of nearly everything, from newspapers to bill posts. Schooling expanded dramatically. Soldiers were issued with written manuals. The written word shaped and was part of this dramatically changing society. As historians Andrew Pettegree and Arthur de Weduwen pithily encapsulate, 'throughout the nineteenth century and well into the next, books, magazines and newspapers were both critical instruments of modernity and its chronicler.'[38] While the range of work expanded and became urbanised, by the second half of the century also saw the introduction of work-time legislation, giving more people the opportunity to find space in the week to read. Some of this demand could be satisfied by British mechanics' institute libraries or the French Bibliothèque des Amis de l'instruction. Higher education underwent a transformation in its use of the printed word. As numbers of students attending college, university and technical institutes increased dramatically, so did the use of texts as teaching tools, all of which helped to stimulate the publishing industry and its commissioning and printing of books. Tutorials and lectures were augmented by reading lists and primers developed into textbooks, particularly in the more vocational subjects, but also in the courses of study such as Classics, which required a selection of set texts. Many new institutions were founded, all with their own library, and existing institutes expanded their older libraries. Holdings increased dramatically in terms of number and range of titles, and in the older institutions, where libraries had been closely guarded spaces, a gradual increase in access began. Opening hours might now be daily, rather than the odd hour here and there.

2.4 Modern Libraries and the Challenges of the Twentieth Century

In an echo of libraries' and publishing's connections to the colonial dissemination and control of information, Pettegree and Weduwen note that 'libraries were not only the victims of war, but were active participants in

---

[38] Pettegree and Weduwen, *The Library*, p. 350.

the conflict': David Lloyd George dubbed the 1914–1918 conflict an 'engineer's war'. While bombing and targeted destruction of industrialised warfare caused a terrible toll on libraries and their stocks in the violent conflicts of the twentieth century, such as that held in Coventry, the scientific and technical knowledge on which such bellicose machinery depended was to be found in the specialised libraries of universities and laboratories (as well as vital information held in the map collections of institutions such as the New York Public Library or the British Museum). Strenuous efforts were undertaken to protect these resources, as well as the national patrimony represented by libraries, with portions of the British Museum's most precious collections, for example, being moved to Aberystwyth in Wales, while collections of scientific literature had been moved to rural locations in the late 1930s, with the hope of saving them from likely bombing raids. Restricting access to the enemy, while still maintaining access to foreign literature was a vital part of the war effort. In Britain, commerce with the Axis was outlawed, but special licences could be obtained, such as that by Cambridge Philosophical Society Library, for example, was granted one for several months and could acquire books via the university library. Booksellers in neutral countries, including Switzerland and, early in the war, the Netherlands, offered another route for supply. In the United States, the Library of Congress' agents were authorised 'to follow the American Army into liberated and occupied areas'. Immediately after the war the Cooperative Acquisitions Program for Wartime Publications, which orchestrated by the Library of Congress, employed twenty-six librarians to screen for marks of ownership and select stock from 'German army and Nazi sources.'[39]

In such ways, libraries attempted to maintain the international flows of the academic book. And such books were in demand. The number of institutions borrowing from the Science Museum Library rose from 450 to over 1,000 by 1945, with chemistry, physics and engineering – fields typically dominated by German publishers – particularly strong (on the public library front, reading for morale proved to be a crucial part of the war

[39] R. B. Downs, 'Wartime Co-Operative Acquisitions', *The Library Quarterly: Information, Community, Policy* 19 (3) 1949, pp. 157–165.

effort, along with the extensive development of libraries and supplies of books for those in the armed services.) The British Central Science Office was established in part to enable the exchange of books and other materials with the United States to contribute to the development of the atomic bomb, along with a broader focus on obtaining and sharing what it could of the preeminent and extensive German technological and scientific literature. Technologies such as microfilming and microphotography were also deployed to attempt to continue the sharing of scientific literature across the Atlantic and a special air link using microfilm was set up between Britain and China. British and American intelligence set up formal channels of communication between them and the Association of Special Libraries and Information Bureaus (ASLIB) – while also paying close attention to copy-right issues.[40]

While the post-war era also included concerted efforts to make amends for such destruction, the Cold War also intensified governments' focus on the importance of scientific and technical information. University education expanded, as did research across the USSR, Western Europe, and America. Books also played their role in the Cold War as weapons of soft power. Both sides of the Cold War invested in public libraries, as evidence of either liberal values or the benefits of the soviet system. (Publishers also found the expansion of the public library system to be a useful revenue stream.) Authors, wittingly or not, were enabled by organisations such as the British Council to promote Western values of liberal democracy, and other aspects of Western culture that it may have been politic to project at home and abroad.[41] Librarians and libraries also assisted in such work, offering advice to Commonwealth and other countries and attempting to

---

[40] Pettegree and Weduwen, *The Library*, p. 324. Cf. P. S. Richards, 'Aslib at War: The Brief but Intrepid Career of a Library Organization as a Hub of Allied Scientific Intelligence 1942–1945', *Journal of Education for Library and Information Science* 29 (4) 1989, pp. 279–296. L. Moholy, 'The Aslib Microfilm Service: The Story of Its Wartime Activities', *Journal of Documentation* 2 (3) 1946, pp. 147–173.

[41] P. S. Richards, 'Cold War Librarianship: Soviet and American Library Activities in Support of National Foreign Policy, 1946–1991', *Libraries & Culture* 36 (1) 2001, pp. 193–203.

counter the 'book gap' in developing nations that the Soviet Union also attempted to fill.[42] On the flip side, library ideals were also challenged by the domestic policies of the Cold War. In the United State, numerous libraries lost their jobs because of actual or supposed Communist sympathies, and in 1950, Ruth Brown, a long-serving librarian in Bartlesville, Oklahoma was fired, with subversive book stock given as the reason; the real cause being her public sympathy for the African-American cause. How to respond to Truman's loyalty pledge for public servants split the American Library Association (ALA).[43]

The Cold War saw a massive funnelling of state money into research undertaken in higher education and other research institutions, enabling librarians to expand their purchasing dramatically, both in terms of monographs and journals; it was a tide that rose most ships: history monographs, for example, more than quadrupled in number between 1920 and 1995.[44] Drawing on collaboration between government and higher education that predated the Cold War, such as the area studies work of the Research and Analysis Branch of the Office of Strategic Studies (the precursor of the CIA), research libraries grew enormously, and scientific and technical publishers expanded their lists, and profits.[45] Libraries became a hugely important market for the academic book, particularly as monograph-dependent humanities enrolments grew alongside the sciences. Thanks to approval programmes and other book supplier programmes, academic books could expect hundreds of orders across thousands of titles. Rather than hope for a few bestsellers, publishers could explore business models whose profits were based on the number different titles that could be

[42] A. Laugesen, 'Librarians, Library Diplomacy, and the Cultural Cold War, 1950–70', in Greg Barnhisel (ed.), *The Bloomsbury Handbook to Cold War Literary Cultures* (Bloomsbury Academic, 2022), pp. 191–206.

[43] Weduwen & Pettegree, *The Library*, pp. 384–385.

[44] Here, the Cold War intensified existing trends, see R. B. Townsend, 'History and the Future of Scholarly Publishing', *Perspectives* 41 (3) 2003, pp. 32–41.

[45] For a survey of work on the Cold War university, see D. Engerman, 'Rethinking Cold War Universities: Some Recent Histories', *Journal of Cold War Studies* 5 (3) 2003, pp. 80–95.

produced. Academics could find an outlet for their research, helping to contribute to the expansion of knowledge, as well as to their research profile and career, and might also be able to serve the academic community through the editorship of a series of books on increasingly specialised subject areas. Eventually, such expansion created a near-existential crisis for libraries, as publishers and academic societies continued to increase the cost of academic journals (known within libraries as 'serials'), individual subscribers fell away, and library funding failed, perhaps inevitably, to keep pace with rising institutional subscription costs (which might be twenty times or more than that of a personal subscription) and expansion in numbers of titles: as one relatively recent analysis of the state of scholarly communications summarises, 'from the 1960s onwards – even as commercial publishers became increasingly dominant – libraries faced increasing financial difficulties. By the 1980s, talk of a 'serials crisis' became widespread'.[46] (Although it might be noted that in 1927 American science librarians reported that the majority of their budgets went on serials.)[47]

Despite these challenges, libraries and higher education remained entwined. Globally, libraries focussing on various aspects of academic experience were central to almost all campuses: an undergraduate library, with extensive study space and textbooks and other recommended reading from course curriculums, a research library with specialised texts and reference works, along with rare book and other special collections, and a host of faculty or other specialist libraries, notably business, law or science

---

[46] Directorate-General for Research and Innovation (European Commission), 'Future of scholarly publishing and scholarly communication: Report of the Expert Group to the European Commission' (Publications Office of the European Union, 2019), retrieved 31 October 2022 from digitalcommons.unl.edu/scholcom/97; G. S. McGuigan and R. D. Russell, 'The Business of Academic Publishing: A Strategic Analysis of the Academic Journal Publishing Industry and Its Impact on the Future of Scholarly Publishing,' *Electronic Journal of Academic and Special Librarianship* 9 (3) 2008, retrieved 31 October 2022 from digitalcommons.unl.edu/ejasljournal/105/.

[47] G. A. Works, *College and University Library Problems: A Study of a Selected Group of Institutions Prepared for the Association of American Universities* (Chicago Library Association, 1927).

libraries. Smaller, less financially secure institutions might only be able to provide a reduced version of such provision, but libraries by the close of the twentieth century – possibly rebadged as a learning centre or other formulation reflecting their centrality to the student experience, and pointing to its function as far more than just a storehouse for books.

In 2022, the International Federation of Library Associations (IFLA) recorded 2.7 million libraries worldwide (the data excludes some countries, notably those in Africa and the Middle East where data is not available). Of these, 2.2 million are school libraries, 407,393 are public libraries and 82,093 are academic libraries (350 national libraries are listed, many of which have similarities to academic libraries). Academic libraries represent a substantial number of the proportion of librarians. Out of 1.6 million library workers, 21.9 per cent are Academic library staff. Academic libraries account for 18.2 per cent of 1,046.8 million registered readers. In terms of use, physical loans are relatively low (9.9 per cent), but dominate electronic loans (90.8 per cent) – a testament to the success of digital journals.[48]

But at the same time, the development of libraries often passes unnoticed elsewhere in the academy. What might we learn from the relative absence of 'library' from histories of higher education? To take one example, a recent architectural and social history of UK 'redbrick' universities does not contain 'library' in the index, although these buildings do appear in the text (not least as a space in which female undergraduates met male ones).[49] It does include the information that Maynooth university's centenary was marked by a comment 'that, whereas we should get fifteen thousand pounds for a tower and spire, we should not get one-fifth of the sum for library endowment'.[50]

---

[48] IFLA, 'Library Map of the World', retrieved 31 October 2022 from librarymap .ifla.org.

[49] W. Whyte, *Redbrick: A Social and Architectural History of Britain's Civic Universities* (Oxford University Press, 2015).

[50] Whyte, *Redbrick*, p. 167.

3 People and Institutions

In 1922, the American librarian Theodore Wesley Koch visited the Leipzig bookfair in post-war Germany. As Director of the Library of Northwestern University, Koch straddled the world of American and European books and libraries. During the First World War, he served on the staff of the Library of Congress, where he ensured that the United States acquired publications from German researchers and organised programmes to provide US soldiers with books. When the war ended he assisted in the rebuilding and restocking of European libraries, and in his later career he worked to stock the new Deering Library. A bibliophile with a penchant for privately printed editions of his works, Koch published a short book on his bookish adventure that began with a justification that such a trip – long before the age of social media, Zoom video conferencing and publisher's online catalogues – was a necessity 'to keep in touch with the state of the European book market.'[51] Koch also leavens this opening with some light humour: 'Incidentally, it is my favourite method of taking a vacation.'

His account, which also includes an account of the rebuilding of the library at Louvain, following its destruction during the War, is germane to many current as well as historical aspects of libraries and the academic book, such as the role of booksellers and matters of finance. The mild joke about Koch's vacation preferences also speaks of a truth, too, or at least a tension. Libraries are complex organisations, with workflows, policies and procedures, all grounded in decades of management and library and information theory, and usually found within an even larger higher education institution. They are also staffed and run by individuals, each with their own tastes, interests and predispositions. For some, this might be a fascination with books as carriers of information, for others, the book as an object and the complex world of authors and publishers that manufacture them might. Others might be concerned more with the building, or the order of the materials kept within

---

[51] T. W. Koch, *The Leipzig Book Fair: Rebuilding the Louvain Library. Travel Sketches from the portfolio of Thomas Wesley Koch* (Privately printed, 1923). The edition was reprinted from Koch's account in the book review section of the *Detroit Free Press*, 29 October, 5 November 1922 and 7 January 1923.

it, or the behaviour or happiness of its readers or patrons. There will also be a mixture of all these, their proportions shifting at various times. While I offer an outline and some analysis in this Element of how libraries and the academic book have changed over the last century, and look at current concerns, this human dimension should always be remembered.

Librarianship

Who, then, staffed and ran the libraries in these institutions? Library workers have of course been central to how libraries operated.[52] As a profession or work activity, librarianship might be counted as an ancient one, which can be traced back to Ashurbanipal, the Assyrian king (668–631 BCE) who amassed a library of over 20,000 clay tablets, and required librarians to organise and catalogue it. The Library of Alexandra included Demetrius of Phalerum, Zenodotus, Aristophanes of Phalerum and Callimachus among its librarians, while the great humanist libraries of Renaissance or Enlightenment Europe included Gottfied Wilhelm Leibniz as a librarian in two major libraries: Hanover and Wolfenbüttel. In 1598, Sir Thomas Bodley refounded the library at the University of Oxford, hiring a librarian, Thomas James, when he did so to work on a catalogue: James's labours were published in 1605 as the Bodleian Library catalogue, the first printed library catalogue (which listed title in shelf-list order; an alphabetical author/title catalogue followed in 1620). We have strong sense that James took things in his own direction, causing Bodley to ask for more involvement: 'I can not choose but impart my fansie unto yow in the smallest maters of the Libr[ary]', Bodley wrote to James in 1602. James has also been credited with the notion of 'legal deposit', helping to arrange the agreement between the Stationers' Company of London and the university that the company would deposit the books it printed in the library.[53]

---

[52] For a suggestive overview, see the timeline in M. E. Quinn, *Historical Dictionary of Librarianship* (Rowman & Littlefield, 2014).

[53] J. R. Roberts, 'James, Thomas (1572/3–1629), librarian and religious controversialist,' *Oxford Dictionary of National Biography*, 23 September 2004, retrieved 23 September 2022 from www.oxforddnb.com/view/10.1093/ref:odnb/9780 198614128.001.0001/odnb-9780198614128-e-14619.

Only later did a sense of 'librarian' as a profession emerge. By the eighteenth century, the term 'librarian' (as opposed to 'library-keeper') came into more common use, but 'librarianship' as a term dates from the early nineteenth century, and the librarian of the Bavarian State Library could write of 'the foundation of library science' during the same period as Friedrich Adolf Ebert (the librarian at Dresden) published his manual *Die Bildung des Bibliothekars* (1820). Ebert believed in the importance of being able to study works in their original languages, as well as the deployment of neat handwriting (a requirement at many libraries in the twentieth century) and, on occasion, carpentry skills in relation to difficult shelves. Most historians suggest that there was much work to be done here, much, summarizees Catherine Minter, 'was amiss in academic libraries in England, France, and Germany in the eighteenth century. Libraries were poorly stocked and badly organised; librarians proved, or else were styled as, idle and unhelpful.' Charles Morton, the Principal Librarian at the British Museum, might be taken as a typical example: 'a man of sedentary habits, extremely idle, disposed to let things run on from day to day and rarely to show the slightest initiative'.

But change was to come. More liberal access to collections was encouraged across Europe from the late eighteenth century. Göttingen university library, for example, was open for a couple of hours a day most days of the week to the public, scarcely something to note compared to today's common 24-hour-opening times, but still enough to encourage comment by a visiting student in 1791. Other libraries began to follow these patterns, creating and responding to demands from a growing readership; the British Museum added under-librarians to its staff after 1799, pointing to increased activity in the reading room.[54] Cataloguing systems and other methods of modern librarianship were developed across Europe during the second half of the nineteenth century, and were introduced most notably in Britain under the leadership of Sir Antony Panizzi at the British Museum, where he was appointed Keeper of Printed Books in 1837 – the year after Museum

[54] C. Minter, 'Academic Library Reform and the Ideal of the Librarian in England, France, and Germany in the Long Nineteenth Century', *Library & Information History* 29 (1) 2021, pp. 19–37.

officers were forbidden from taking positions elsewhere at the same time, effectively ending the roles as sinecures (the Bibliothèque nationale in Paris introduced the same strictures later that century). He directed his assistant to prepare a cataloguing code dealing with such matters as how to list anonymous authors, increased the annual book fund, and developed services for readers. Panizzi's colleague and assistant cataloguer, Edward Edwards, became a spokesman for the public library movement, publishing in 1847 'Public libraries in London and Paris' in *The British Quarterly Review*. His campaigning, which came at a time of parliamentary scrutiny of the British Museum, helped to spark the great development in public libraries from the 1850s following William Ewart MP's Public Library Act (Edwards would leave the Museum under a cloud – in part for using BM stationary to write to foreign libraries – and took up posts at the Salford Public Library and then the Manchester Free Public Library).

In February 1853, *Morton's Literary Gazette* included a call for a librarian's conference, noting that 'hundreds of libraries more or less public, mercantile, mechanic, social, collegiate and state, are already in vigorous operation, new enterprises are constantly started, and as one after another of our West cities spring up to rival its Eastern predecessors, the Library is regularly to hold no unimportant place among the public undertakings'. The meeting did not result in an association immediately – something that would wait until 1876 and the founding of the American Library Association – but points to the self-identification of librarianship as a profession, with shared concerns, aims and tasks. Librarianship was seen to encompass all types of libraries, from small public libraries to major university repositories, encompassing a huge variety of tasks and approaches to the role. Common threads in librarianship were drawn together in the curriculum of the first library school (the School of Library Economy), founded by Melvil Dewey at Columbia in New York in January 1887, which admitted women as well as men from its inauguration; indeed, the library profession benefitted from the numbers of women entering the clerical and semi-professional labour market. In the United Kingdom, the Library Association was founded in 1877 (and in 1879, the British Museum published the first national union catalogue). Informal library training continued to be an important route into the profession, and indeed remained so in the United Kingdom.[55]

The impetus for the development of public libraries managed to combine political radicals' belief in the importance of education as a route to improvement with a more conservative interest in the moral benefits of appropriate reading. These amalgam helped with the founding of new libraries and the expansion of existing ones. Imported via the Young Men's Christian Association and mechanics institutes, libraries also spread in the United States of America. The Boston Athenaeum employed women its staff in 1857, with Harvard following two years later. Librarians also drew on European and British experience; the librarian of the Mercantile Association of New York visited in 1855, and Lewis H. Steiner, the librarian of the Enoch Pratt Free Library, undertook a tour in 1884 – his son, his successor as librarian, did the same in 1892.

The librarian of the American Antiquarian Society, Christopher Columbus Baldwin, encapsulated one approach to collecting, declaring that 'I have proposed to myself the task of forming in our library a perfect collection of every book and pamphlet ever made in this country'. This view of comprehensive national collecting was a view shared by many libraries and historical societies at the time. The library historian Kenneth E. Carpenter reminds us that the goal of a universal library was not only one shared by many across Europe in the nineteenth century (and was one of Panizzi's aims for the British Museum) but was one that was interpreted in a particular American way, as an assertion of national identity and 'even to provide antiquity in an era in which age legitimized'. Others, of course, also made other arguments, notably that American libraries did not need every book, but needed *good* books. In building American libraries, a range of methods were used. Many collections arrived, of course, via donation, but librarians were also empowered to purchase materials from time to time.

---

[55] S. K. Vann, *Training for Librarianship before 1923: Education for Librarianship Prior to the Publication of Williamson's Report on Training for Library Service* (American Library Association, 1961). See also F. L. Miksa, 'The Columbia School of Library Economy, 1887–1888', *Libraries & Culture* 23 (3) 1988, pp. 249–280.

Harvard allowed two of its professors, George Ticknor and Henry Wadsworth Longfellow to Europe to acquire books while they were abroad. In 1859, Harvard established a Library Committee with funds to purchase new books, and libraries across America expanded their purchasing of new books in the late 1860s, typically via books on approval from booksellers or at public auction. External consultants were also on hand, notable William Frederick Poole – of *Poole's Index* fame, who advised ten libraries, mostly on selecting books, between 1869 and 1873. Library suppliers, such as the Boston firm Lockwood, Brooks, & Company could provide lists of books, as well as bookcases and other library materials.[56]

A growing cohort of librarians began to select, acquire, catalogue and make available books. A tension, as historians of libraries have detailed, was always apparent in such undertakings between the desire to acquire 'good books' and books that readers wished to read, a tension that was also apparent in the library movement in the UK. Academic books, it might be assumed, fell into the former category, but not necessarily in the latter. While many civic or private libraries did have important stocks of academic works, such as the Westminster Reference Library or The London Library, the more specialised academic book was far less common in the general public library system, particularly as that marketplace developed and matured in the twentieth century. Tensions in book selection in academic libraries might instead be found between the institution's academics and the librarians. Who chose the books? Librarians working from suppliers' lists, or academics working from their own knowledge and course reading lists? Academics might lack the time or inclination to select books, as well as current understanding of the publishing sector, while librarians might not possess the necessary subject or pedagogic experience to select suitable texts. Library committees were often the solution to these potential tensions, or at least the formal means of dealing with them, and the development of subject specialist academic librarians can be seen as one way of resolving this issue, with greater or lesser degrees of success. Studies of these relationships indeed draw attention to some of the problems, notably a lack of understanding of the work of librarians: as one 2017 study notes,

---

[56] K. E. Carpenter, *Readers & Libraries* (Library of Congress, 1996), pp. 15–22.

'many of the issues that impede effective collections development stem from the different operational and communicative cultures that exist within academia, particularly between those of academic staff and librarians'. Conflict over the 'financial pie' is another.[57] However, the vast increase in the number of books acquired by libraries in the post-war years point to the effectiveness in shifting selection from academics and curators to librarians, a solution forced, by the 'sheer volume of decisions' confronting libraries such as Cornell, Harvard, Yale, or Stanford, which first appointed teams of 'academically and bibliographically trained librarians to coordinate the selection and acquisition process'. It was a 'practice that multiplied quickly.'[58] More recently, librarians, academics and others have engaged with student interest in more diverse, decolonised selection practices.

3.1 Service

Librarians' roles had expanded from the mid nineteenth century from 'caretakers of books' into educators and 'collection promoters'.[59] This change was the cause of a good deal of self-reflection within the profession. In 1889, for example, the Principal Librarian of the British Museum Edward Maunde Thompson declared that the days of being 'only a keeper of books' are 'fled forever'. In Germany, librarians were expected to be focussed on their readers, and the University of Göttingen's librarian Johann Matthias Gesner's advice in his treatise on librarianship 'Wie ein *Bibliothecarius* beschaffen seyn müsse' (itself dating from 1748) was often quoted as an ideal of a nineteenth-century librarian-type:

---

[57] C. Cameron and G. Siddall, 'Opening Lines of Communication: Book Ordering and Reading Lists, the Academics View', *New Review of Academic Librarianship* 23 (1) 2017, pp. 42–59.

[58] H. Edleman, 'The Growth of Scholarly and Scientific Libraries', in R. E. Abel and L. W. Newlin (eds.), *Scholarly Publishing: Books, Journals, Publishers, and Libraries in the Twentieth Century* (Wiley, 2002), p. 199.

[59] J. C. Fagan, H. Ostermiller, E. Price, and L. Sapp, 'Librarian, Faculty, and Student Perceptions of Academic Librarians: Study Introduction and Literature Review', *New Review of Academic Librarianship* 27 (1) 2021, pp. 38–75.

'a congenial and sociable man, not a pedant or curmudgeon'.[60] It was during this period that another tension in the librarian's role was made visible, that of the impulses of a scholar and the requirements of a librarian. In a paper delivered at the annual meeting of the Library Association of Great Britain in Cambridge in 1882, Henry Richard Tedder noted strongly that 'a finished scholar or accomplished specialist may often turn out a very incompetent person to have charge of a library'.[61]

Minter concludes that

> Academic librarians of the nineteenth century in England, France, and Germany cannot be accused of having failed to move with the times. On the contrary, they embraced multiplying service and technical responsibilities; new roles also gave definition to a new professional image, comprised of virtues such as conscientiousness, courtesy, self-effacement, self-sacrifice, and dedication.

Such self-effacement risked a diminishment in status, since, 'the handmaiden of scholarship, does not necessarily foster professional self-esteem.'[62] Perhaps some of these attitudes are an inevitable consequence of a library's efficient operation. In contrast to the monograph, which makes a splash for its academic author, the library worker's achievement is when they are The librarian Catherine not noticed; after all, as one study of academics' information behaviours concludes, 'scholars need systems that support their interactions without complicating them.'[63] Minter also reminds us that

> in an attempt to prove equal standing within the academic environment, librarians tend to trumpet their prowess as traditional scholars, while downplaying their uniqueness as

---

[60] Quoted in Minter, 'Academic Library Reform', p. 34.

[61] Quoted in Minter, 'Academic Library Reform', p. 34.

[62] Quoted in Minter, 'Academic Library Reform', p. 34.

[63] N. Falciani-White, 'Information Behaviors of Elite Scholars in the Context of Academic Practice', *Journal of Documentation* 73 (5) 2017, pp. 953–973.

trusted assessor. As a corollary, librarians obscure their substantial role in contributing to intellectual networks on their respective campuses and across the globe.[64]

One of these contributions was a range of research, notably policy work. The twentieth century also built on a vital development in the Victorian era: the development of research by librarians. Guides such as Naudé's, as long-lasting as they were, and based on individual experience, were works of individuals. Scholar librarians, or reformers such as Panizzi, tended to impose their own vision on an institution. Yet, work such as that of Edwards, who attempted to quantify the provision and potential of libraries and which were profoundly influential in the reform and development of libraries in the mid-nineteenth century (even as the quality of his work was attacked by detractors), pointed to the importance of evidence-based policy work and change. Quantitative and qualitative research by librarians and library organisations have been crucial in shaping the debates around open access and library provision, as the head of higher education and science at the British Library, Maja Maricevic has noted, and this points to the crucial role played by many librarians in a range of research communities and networks, notably in the field of digital humanities.[65] The importance of research was not just demonstrated by men such as Edwards but also, as the information historian Kate McDowell has shown, was developed by women, crucially by qualitative surveys created by librarians promoting services for children and published as *Reading of the Young* reports at the ALA conferences between 1882 and 1898. These methods became the model

---

[64] J. Finnell, 'Much Obliged: Analyzing the Importance and Impact of Acknowledgements in Scholarly Communication', *Library Philosophy and Practice (e-journal)* (paper 1229) 2014, retrieved 6 November 2022 from eprints .rclis.org/25428/1/Finnell_Much%20Obliged.pdf.

[65] M. Maricevic, 'National Libraries and Academic Books of the Future', in R. E. Lyons and S. J. Rayner (eds.), *The Academic Book of the Future* (Palgrave Macmillan, 2016), pp. 57–65; J. Hagerlid, 'The Role of the National Library as a Catalyst for an Open Access Agenda: The Experience of Sweden', *Interlending and Document Supply* 39 (2) 2011, pp. 115–118.

for much future research by librarians, and the basis for the development of scientific, professional librarianship in the twentieth century. Indeed, until recently, it was easy to forget that such research drew on the experiences of women, both in their prior experience of using surveys and in their need to organise and work together in the face of a male profession (it should be noted without the presence of women on Dewey's course, for example, it would be unlikely to have survived) Similarly, the research by women changed how librarianship was done: 'when women entered the discourse of librarianship, they altered the field substantially, introducing a research model that blended previously separated evidence based on individual expertise and gathering statistics.'[66] As Mary Niles Maack notes: 'Historians cannot hope to arrive at an understanding of women's role in librarianship without greater attention to those areas where women proved themselves innovative and resourceful, despite lack of broad recognition or high status'.[67]

3.2 The Modern Library Profession

The history of librarianship in the twentieth century is too large a topic for this Element. But in terms of the relationship between the library and the academic book, several strands can be stressed during this period of dramatic expansion in terms of numbers, roles, and responsibilities; the rise of international collaboration; and professionalisation. Clearly, specialisation is one important theme. The split between public and academic librarianship became more pronounced through the century, even while the commonalities in terms of values and practices have continued to be stressed in library schools. Within academic libraries, specialisation has been increasingly pronounced, with career paths following routes into serial or monograph acquisitions and cataloguing, technical services, reference services, and

---

[66] K. McDowell, 'Surveying the Field: The Research Model of Women in Librarianship, 1882–1898', *The Library Quarterly* 79 (3) 2009, pp. 279–300.

[67] M. Bianco, 'Academia Is quietly and systematically keeping Its women from succeeding', QZ, 30 April 2016, retrieved 6 November 2022 from qz.com/670647/academia-is-quietly-and-systematically-keeping-its-women-from-succeeding.

academic liaison or subject specialisms.[68] Librarianship as an academic discipline, sharing approaches from the social sciences, computer science, and business studies, has also become increasingly embedded in library and information schools, creating a set of theories to understand how information is used and analysing what libraries do or how they might function. Within the discipline, a debate continues about the focus on theory versus vocational change, and library school programmes tend to emphasise one or the other of these foci.[69] Libraries themselves also tended towards specialisation: undergraduate libraries, science libraries, law libraries. All have had a different approach to the academic book: undergraduate libraries, for example, deal in multiple copies, textbooks, and regular weeding, and present a long-term market for publishers. More specialist libraries attempt to collect an advanced level from established university presses, but also need more specialist connections and acquisitions programmes to acquire from more specialist, smaller publishers, perhaps those that focus on classical or area studies, and, especially, works in foreign languages. Profits here may be more modest for publishers, leaving the field to smaller, more nimble or perhaps charitable publishers. There is, it might be noted, the potential for librarians to have very little to do with books as their career progresses.

3.3 Academics and Other Readers

The same may be true, of course, of some academics, particularly in the sciences, whose publications are online or in journal format. Materials may appear on their laptops without, as far as they are aware, any intervention by a librarian. But for the majority of academics, books remain important, even if visits to the library are fewer than they once were, and with some research pointing to the possibility of increased serendipitous discovery in

---

[68] J. V. Martin, 'Subject Specialization in British University Libraries: A Second Survey', *Journal of Librarianship and Information Science* 28 (3) 1996, pp. 159–169.
[69] R. Audunson, 'Library and Information Science Education — Discipline Profession, Vocation?', *Journal of Education for Library and Information Science* 48 (2) 2007, pp. 94–107; B. P. Lynch, 'Library Education: Its Past, Its Present, Its Future', *Library Trends* 56 (4) 2008, pp. 931–953.

physical stacks compared to online searching.[70] But patterns of use have changed dramatically in the first decades of the twenty-first century, something on which the historian and digital humanist and Andrew Prescott reflected as part of the British Library's The Academic Book of the Future project:

> I've acquired many academic books over the years, but I suspect that for academic books this was more often than not a means of possessing books or authors I particularly admired, almost as trophies, rather than for use. I have always preferred to work in libraries, and have been lucky enough to either work in libraries or live in close proximity to major libraries, so my working copies of academic books tend to be library copies.

Prescott notes that his use has changed, particularly in relation to articles. The arrival of a new tablet device was a revelation, however:

> I had acquired an iPad a few months earlier, and decided that the pain in my back necessitated a switch to an e-book, and acquired Edward III as an e-biography. It was one of the greatest revelations of my life. It wasn't just that I no longer had to lumber around that huge brick of ink, paper and card, although that was a great relief. The clarity of the screen and the backlighting seemed somehow to make it easier to connect the book and for me definitely made the reading experience more intense. Far from the iPad getting in the

[70] S. Brown, 'Researchers' use of academic libraries and their services: A report commissioned by the Research Information Network and the Consortium of Research Libraries' (2007), retrieved 6 November 2022 from eprints.soton.ac.uk/263868/1/libraries-report-2007.pdf. L. Björneborn, 'Serendipity Dimensions and Users' Information Behaviour in the Physical Library Interface', *Information Research* 13 (4) (2008), retrieved on 11 November 2023 from informationr.net/ir/13–4/paper370.html.

way, I seemed to be able to connect with the e-book much more easily.[71]

Many academic authors will also develop their own personal library, created from books gathered during graduate study, donations from friends, colleagues, or former students, examination copies and works sent for review, as well as through serendipitous discovery.[72] Many institutions, but by no means all, also provide book-purchasing funds as part of research money or part of project funds from grant-making bodies. Academics will have their own, unwritten collection development policy, too. The more bibliophilic may acquire with as much fever as the nineteenth-century bibliophiles skewered by Thomas Frognall Dibdin in his *Bibliomania, or Book Madness* (1809) and described by the French librarian and writer Charles Nodier, who in 'The Book Collector' (1841) distinguished between discerning bibliophiles and a bibliomaniacs who 'hoard and amass them'. For such scholars, might research agendas might be shaped (perhaps even distorted) by chance finds in books seller's carts on the left bank. Others might be more systematic, with collections created for current projects after a systematic bibliography is drawn up, and then discarded once the work is complete. Others might question the need – or perhaps more importantly – given the rise of hotdesking for academics and the housing crisis more generally – the practicality of a large collection of printed books. Strict 'one in; one out' personal (or partner-imposed) acquisition policies might be enforced, or collections may move to e-books, whether Kindle or downloads of PDFs of chapters derived from university library-curated (and licenced) collections.

---

[71] A. Prescott, 'My Acts of Reading', The Academic Book of the Future, retrieved 6 November 2022 from academicbookfuture.org/2015/03/19/my-acts-of-reading-andrew-prescott.

[72] See S. Antonijević and E. Stern Cahoy, 'Personal Library Curation: An Ethnographic Study of Scholars' Information Practices', *Portal: Libraries and the Academy* 14 (2) 2014, pp. 287–306.

Such practical questions always challenged scholars, even as they sought to find dry spaces to store valuable books in medieval colleges. They continue to have a harsh, modern edge. Academia can be a very precarious and often inequitable profession, especially for early career researchers (a period which may extend to unfeasible lengths). A University and College Union (UCU) motion in 2019 modelled on work at UCU Senate House, University of London, called for higher education institutions to support early career researchers and recent graduates with library access following graduation or at the end of their contract, to enable them to continue their research – necessary for building an employable curriculum vitae.[73] Lack of access to remote digital library resources remains a common complaint. Physical access to libraries, and even loaning of materials, is more easily achievable, and is something that takes place for graduates of Oxford and Cambridge, as well as many civic universities. Local access to libraries is a common aspect of state universities in the United States, for example. However, access to electronic resources is a much more complicated issue. Items are licenced only for current staff and students, and even if there is the time to renegotiate terms, there is often a likely imposing financial cost to library budgets. There are, of course, successful models for this sort of access – JSTOR, for example, offers an alumni package via many universities, although this is often a subset of the entire collection. One wonders what such access might look like as more libraries move to a digital-first monograph purchasing policy.

Today's generation of students are experiencing this as part of their education, one of the earliest cohorts to do so. Students, we should note, have had a varied relationship with scholarly books and libraries, often a slightly painful one. Indeed, students often had little to do with libraries. To take one example, until the twentieth century, at The Queen's College, Oxford, students were given very limited access to the library, with half an hour being considered sufficient, and this was at a college with an

---

[73] 'Passed motion: Post-contract support for precarious academic contracts, 20 February 2019, Senate House UCU', retrieved 6 November 2022 from ucu .london.ac.uk/2019/02/20/passed-motion-post-contract-support-for-precar ious-academic-contracts.

unusually generous provision for undergraduates, with a dedicated 'Taberdars' library'. Reliance on other teaching methods was common for students, no matter where they studied. One student recalled 'books, outside of text-books used, had no part in our education.'[74] This might be a comment on teaching methods, with lectures and tutorials, rather than individual study, forming the bedrock of education at that time. In contrast to the student use of texts, portraits of provosts from the seventeenth century and later that are displayed around the college usually depict the sitter holding a book, often open in their hand, a visual trope that is rarer in portraits from the nineteenth century onwards. Students at colleges and universities in the United State before the Civil War relied on student society libraries, rather than negotiate the small stock and limited hours and lending practices of institutional libraries. In New England, such societies even created a joint book society.[75] Students today might happily accept half-an-hour access to pulling printed books from the shelves, but would be in uproar if access to digital texts through online readings lists were unavailable (and would similarly protest if access to a library as a space to use their laptops did not extend around the clock, or at least most of the day). We might also reflect on the different ways that books are used. What would a university education be without the cross-cohort conversation (or banter) engendered by generations of marginalia, some earnest, some incredibly crude – and also of increasing interest to historians of the book. Digital annotations rarely seem to capture the same spirit, if they are possible at all.

The role of books in education is by no means one that is a static or certain, either in terms of its actual use and representation. Indeed, the current cohort of students are guinea pigs for 'e-first' collections, in which monographs are purchased as electronic copies in the first instance, with great discrepancies of access depending on the wealth of the institution and the individual, given that libraries licences for such works can be

---

[74] Quoted in Koch, *On University Libraries*, p. 25.

[75] E. D. Johnson, *History of Libraries in the World* (Scarecrow Press, 1970), n. 4, pp. 315, 336, cited in C. A. Brock, 'Introduction: Why Networks for Libraries?', *Law Library Journal* 70 (1) 1977, p. 54.

prohibitive.[76] Libraries beyond the academy should not be forgotten in this survey. Indeed, for many autodidacts, public or other civic libraries were their only access to scholarly works. Indeed, unexpected outcomes have often been sparked by the presence of academic books in public libraries. The image on page 111 of *The Cambridge Encyclopaedia of Astronomy* showing 'successive pulses from the first pulsar discovered, CP1919' inspired Bernard Sumner of the band Joy Division, who gave the image to Peter Saville as the basis for the cover design of their album *Unknown Pleasures.* Sumner had taken to visiting the library during his lunch break nearby, seeking inspiration.[77] The Astor Library in New York (1839), the forerunner of the New York Public Library, and the Boston Public Library (1852) offered the riches of a great research library to all. The research library exists, we should remember, beyond academia. Readers could also, eventually, benefit from the collecting passions of the robber barons at the Newberry, the Huntington and the Morgan libraries. Similarly, student readers are not all of one bloc, and the image of the student as an eighteen to twenty-one or twenty-two-year-old does not capture the reality. Even this stereotype is wrong, for example, in the 1950s, a large number Oxbridge undergraduates had undertaken military or National Service and began their degrees at twenty-one or older. Elsewhere, correspondence courses accounted for huge numbers of the total of those studying. Mature students were increasingly represented, and night schools. In the United States, the G.I. Bill profoundly transformed the higher education landscape. Elsewhere, student numbers expanded also, notably in post-1968 France. A range of higher educations, in parallel to apprenticeships. But the dominant model, drawing on German, American and British systems of three or four years-long

---

[76] R. Hotten, 'University Staff Urge Probe into E-book Pricing "Scandal"', *BBC News*, 13 November 2020, retrieved 6 November 2022 from www.bbc.co.uk/news/business-54922764.

[77] J. Christiansen, 'Pop Culture Pulsar: Origin Story of Joy Division's Unknown Pleasures Album Cover', *Scientific American*, 18 February 2015, retrieved 6 November 2022 from blogs.scientificamerican.com/sa-visual/pop-culture-pulsar-origin-story-of-joy-division-s-unknown-pleasures-album-cover-video.

undergraduate degrees and postgraduates following one to two years-long masters and longer doctoral programmes. Access to books for these groups suggests a whole host of other types of reading.

3.4 Publishers

'Publishers,' Sir Stanley Unwin (of George, Allen & Unwin) noted, 'are not necessarily either philanthropists or rogues'.[78] Like librarians they are gate-keepers and protectors of knowledge and, as the historian Jane Morley notes, 'guardians of written culture'.[79] Treading a path between profit and publishing for the public good, their relationship with the academic book and libraries is a key part of this story. It is also, like libraries, one of variety. Scientific publishing and publishing in the arts, humanities, and social sciences, took different routes, and ones that might be best understood in national terms. While most of this Element has focussed on Britain and America – but has attempted to be alert to the academic book in other contexts – scholarly publishing is a northern European phenomenon as well as a transatlantic one. Presses in German and the Netherlands, notably Springer and Elsevier (unconnected to the printing family of Elzevier) It is a story that emphasises the growing importance of journals, and the power of scholarly societies, notably the Royal Society, that were particularly important for the publication of scientific material. As the writers of the important 2022 history of publishing at the Royal Society note, 'for scientific authors, publication in the pages of the *Transactions*, and other journals like it, came to carry far more social capital than it had formerly done.' The quirky seventeenth-century origins of the *Transactions* and its staid memoirs of gentleman amateurs of the eighteenth century was able, perhaps surprisingly, to adapt to the professionalisation of science from the 1820s, and its need for speedier, shorter communication.[80] North American societies, including the American

---

[78] S. Unwin, *The Truth about Publishing* (George Allen & Unwin, 1950), p. 19.

[79] J. Morley, 'Publishers and Librarians: A Foundation for Dialogue. Mary Biggs', *Isis* 76 (4) 1985, p. 25.

[80] A. Fyfe, N. Moxham, J. McDougall-Waters, and C. Mørk Røstvik, *A History of Scientific Journals: Publishing at the Royal Society, 1665–2015* (UCL Press, 2022), p. 12.

Economic Association (1885), the American Chemical Society (1876) and the American Mathematical Society (1888), all developed important journals. In contrast, the majority of American university presses were often 'served as no more than job printers for universities, printing catalogues, unvetted faculty publications or annual reports'. Between 1934 and 1941, for example, the University of California press only published around a dozen books a year. As the communications professor Albert Greco suggests, academic publishing was dominated by a small number of university presses and professional societies before the late 1940s, with perhaps the majority of texts used in higher education published by trade firms. However, the Second World War disrupted the dominance of German scientific presses, which had witnessed substantial consolidation following the First World War. Commercial firms had begun to erode the tradition of not-for-profit publishing, and many émigré publishers, bringing this experience with them, founded English-language houses, such as Academic Press and Michael Dekker. Indeed, English became the post-war lingua-franca of scientific publishing at firms such as Elsevier. Springer's *Pflügers Archiv – European Journal of Physiology* began publishing in English after more than 300 volumes in German.[81]

From the 1930s, university presses had begun to transform their operation. Smaller university presses formed the Association of University Presses (AUUP), and presses as a whole began to behave more competitively. The 'conglomerate phenomenon' of the post-war era saw the creation of a smaller number of big publishers, which were then able to use their size and scale to increase the number of books and journals published, acquire the publishing rights to the field-dominating journals of major professional societies, create new book series and journals devoted to subfields (a process known as 'twigging' in publishing). Continued global expansion of the higher education sector encouraged publishers to launch online platforms to uncover their content in the digital age. Much of the financing of this expansion came via library budgets and unpaid (or at least

---

[81] Richard E. Abel and Lyman W. Newlin, *Scholarly Publishing: Books, Journals, Publishers, and Libraries in the Twentieth Century* (John Wiley & Sons, 2002).

not directly paid) academic labour.[82] Larger presses, such as Oxford, Cambridge, Harvard, Yale, Princeton, California, or Chicago were able to compete with commercial scholarly conglomerates due to their size and reputation. Smaller university presses had to rely on the prestige that they could bring to the publishing process, and their editorial staff's close connection to academics and the discipline; university libraries are less price conscious than general consumers; selection is instead made on the basis of subject matter, the reputation of the author (and the publisher) and how up to date it is, especially in the scientific, technical and medical fields. Most purchases are also via library suppliers, such as Library Solutions which in 2019 accounted for 68.7 per cent of a sample of major academic libraries in the United States ($17,723,700).[83]

Academics of course have important relationship with publishers in that they are not just consumers of texts, but their writers. Occasionally, this might bring financial reward, as Sir Stanley Unwin's anecdote suggests:

> One such author, the sales of whose masterpiece had taken thirty years to cover the printing bill, called the day after he had received the first share of profits to tell me that it was an amusing coincidence that the payment should have reached him on the very day of his retirement from the Professorship the publication of the book had secured him. (The patient publisher had been out of pocket for over thirty years without any comparable recognition of his part in such uncommercial activities.)[84]

More often, academics find themselves out of pocket, having to pay for research materials, devote their time, pay for reproduction fees for illustrations and perhaps employ a professional indexer, all for a very small or non-existent fee, or a number of free copies of their text. Of course, the

[82] A. N. Greco, *The Business of Scholarly Publishing: Managing in Turbulent Times* (Oxford Academic, 2020), pp. 4–5.

[83] Greco, *Scholarly Publishing*, pp. 99–100.

[84] Unwin, *The Truth about* Publishing, p. 65.

importance of the text – beyond the satisfaction of seeing it in print and the contribution to knowledge – is the prestige that might accrue from publication and, quite possibly, promotion or some job security. After all, the benefits of promotion from lecturer to senior lecture on the partial basis of a good publication, may well far outweigh all but the most generous trade advances over a career, particularly if pension benefits are included. For the publisher, the established market of the academic library makes this financial undertaking possible, along with profits on the rare bestseller, textbooks, or other financial props, such as the university's underwriting of some university presses. Academics also act as keepers and help to bring prestige to publishers' outputs, vetting and editing texts and participating in peer review, usually on an unpaid basis. Libraries, as analyses of the industry note, are also 'important participants in the industry' as purchasers of the final product. Libraries also make these works discoverable through library cataloguing systems (which also often relies on purchasing metadata from publishers) and, ultimately, physically and digitally available to readers.[85] Librarians, much as Koch did, continue to recognise the interconnectedness of academia, librarianship and publishing, and how the balance of power and financial muscle might change over time, while also keeping an eye – as did Sir Stanley – on the ultimate end of sharing information and advancing knowledge.

[85] G. S. McGuigan and R. D. Russell, 'The Business of Academic Publishing: A Strategic Analysis of the Academic Journal Publishing Industry and Its Impact on the Future of Scholarly Publishing,' *E-JASL: The Electronic Journal of Academic and Special Librarianship* 9 (3) 2008, 2.

4 Networks and Scholarly Communications

4.1 The Research Process

How does a book get written? Samuel Johnson famously opined that it takes a library to make a book. It might also take a laboratory, observatory, field research, or serious time spent with a powerful computer for a scientific work, or far-flung archives for a work of history, yet all these endeavours depend on the information, contextualisation and fact-checking of a library, whether analogue or digital. Libraries, I want to argue, play an important role in the research process, and in particular the production and use of academic books. There has been extensive research on the research process – indeed it is its own research field – much of it from a library perspective. In broad terms, we might classify such studies into three types. Firstly, works that attempt to describe the research process, usually within a particular discipline or field of study, as a training tool for new researchers. There is a focus on the stages through which research is undertaken, underpinned by the methodological disciplinary assumptions, such as the scientific methods. Such works may spend time on issues such as ethics or bias and also detail note making and data gathering methodologies. The process of writing a thesis or book, and seeing it through to publication might also be covered in such texts, again with a disciplinary bent and with tips offered along the way. A second class of material draws on techniques from various disciplines, including of sociology or information studies, to explore the wider meaning and context of scholarship, notably the importance of power relationships within academia. A raft of more partisan texts, which seek to reframe, reform, or even 'save' the research process, perhaps by reverting to older methods, adopting new ones, or by making extensive use of new technologies constitute a third group. Many of these interventions also make the case for open access, open data, and 'open scholarship' more broadly.[86]

It is something of a truism, supported by some research, that academics tend to stick with the research methodologies that they were taught as

---

[86] G. Bouma and S. Carland, *The Research Process* (Oxford University Press, 2016).

graduate students.[87] As the historian Sir Keith Thomas noted, 'Nobody gave me any such instructions when I began research in the 1950s. I read neither Beatrice Webb nor Langlois and Seignobos until many years later, by which time my working habits had ossified ... My methods are in no way an advance on those of Burckhardt and now appear impossibly archaic. But it is far too late to think of transferring this accumulation onto some electronic database.'[88] Many academics rely on tried and trusted methods of finding books using simple searches on library catalogues, the reviews sections or works received by certain journals in the field.

Views of academics might still follow the following quotes from an extensive survey of research processes:

- A well-stocked library (including e-materials) is absolutely essential to all aspects of scholarly activity. I can think of no other feasible alternative (54-year-old-female social sciences lecturer).
- Accessibility of scholarly journals and other library resources is crucial to the standing and effectiveness of a university and is a key discriminator between world-class universities and less prestigious institutions (56-year-old-male professor).
- Never visit the library these days. I do all my searching on-line. Time to divert library resources (57-year-old-male medical sciences professor).[89]

As this survey suggests, research is a very individual process, as well has having distinct disciplinary differences; different approaches to library use lead to different forms of scholarship. As such, it is can be useful to bring to bear personal reflections on the research process. Thomas, for example, reflected on the importance of extensive feasting of library materials in the *London Review of Books* Diary (2010).[90] In this wide-ranging account of his

---

[87] B. Gunter, I. Rowlands, and D. Nicholas, *The Google Generation: Are ICT Innovations Changing Information Seeking Behaviour?* (Chandos, 2009).

[88] K. Thomas, 'Working Methods', *London Review of Books*, 10 June 2010, retrieved 6 November 2022 from www.lrb.co.uk/the-paper/v32/n11/keith-thomas/diary.

[89] R. Volentine and C. Tenopir, 'Value of Academic Reading and Value of the Library in Academics' Own Words', *Aslib Proceedings* 65 (4) 2013, pp. 425–440.

[90] Thomas, 'Working Methods'.

approach to the reading and thinking underpinning his writing, Thomas provides details on the specifics of research, particularly the use of envelopes for storing and sorting research notes – despite Thomas worrying that 'just as the conjuror's magic disappears if the audience knows how the trick is done, so the credibility of scholars can be sharply diminished if readers learn everything about how exactly their books came to be written.' As well as a reminder of the human labour and intellectual expertise required to gather information from a library or archive, Thomas's Diary is also a reminder of the imprint physical space has on the ability to undertake scholarly work, reminding us of the need for different kinds of places at different moments in the research process. In his memoir of a life in the historical profession, Patrick Collinson also provides a telling account of physically moving between different libraries and making use of different opening times (heading to the Institute of Historical Research (IHR) in Senate House after the Library of the British Museum closed next door) in his memoir, and quotes Geoffrey Barraclough (with whom Thomas also agrees): 'I had no "method", only an omnium gatherum of materials culled from more or less everywhere.'[91] The Royal College of Art's Living Library project (2010), for example, highlighted the different types of spaces required at various points along the research journey, noting 'the importance that researchers place on the type of space used during the 'create' phase of research, when they are focused on producing outputs. At this stage they often seek a change of environment, preferring a quiet yet atmospheric space more conducive to concentration.' Well-stocked libraries provide another useful location at the time when references in a text are being check, while their cafés and more social areas help to stimulate new research or make connections with colleagues, and even across disciplines.[92]

These examples of library use, taken from the humanities – indeed, from historians – no doubt speaks of a particular understanding of the research process from one point in time, and one that is only very partially representative

[91] Thomas, 'Working Methods'.
[92] 'Living Library: Settings for access and sharing in the knowledge economy', retrieved 6 November 2022 from www.rca.ac.uk/research-innovation/research-centres/helen-hamlyn-centre/research-projects/2010-projects/living-library.

of the kind of work that results in monographs in the modern academy. In Britain, much has changed from the 1950s, when historians fortunate enough to receive a junior research fellowship could make their way between the British Museum and the IHR (and its tea room), supplemented by trips to the Public Record Office in Chancery Lane. It is probably fair to say that there was less of a necessary link between an academic job and an extensive publishing record compared to the influence of a candidate's supervisor. As any workshop on academic careers will stress today, such days are long past (even if the ease of obtaining an academic post in the 1950s and 1960s may well be exaggerated, and the difficulties in the UK in the 1980s are often glossed over).[93] While many academics published prodigious amounts, many more were less productive in terms of publications; current publishing patterns in academia reflect a very different picture. The same pattern has been repeated elsewhere, and throughout academia, the demand for a publishing record (along with a strong dossier on teaching, service, or, in the United Kingdom and to some extent the United States, grant capture) have intensified. Increased output, both mapped in the United Kingdom by the Research Assessment Exercise and then the Research Excellent Framework (REF). Monographs might have been linked to doctoral dissertations with subsequent works perhaps, based on a series of lectures rather than extensive fieldwork, but are now tied to research with, in REF 2021 terms, 'significance', 'rigour,' and 'originality', and remain a significant part of national research output in the humanities (in the 2021 REF covering 2014–2021, 19,182 of assessed outputs were books or parts of books in panel D (54 per cent), versus 11, 765 articles (34 per cent)). In 2019, 19 per cent of monographs were co-authored within the humanities and social sciences, according to a survey undertaken by the university presses of Oxford and Cambridge. By far the majority of academics (69 per cent) had authored one monograph (and 93 per cent had authored a journal article). Thirty-nine per cent had published between two and eight monographs (17 per cent published two). Ninety-one per cent considered monographs to be 'very' or 'extremely' important to the

---

[93] T. Hitchcock, 'Twenty Five Years of the REF and Me', *Historyonics*, retrieved 6 November 2022 from historyonics.blogspot.com/2018/. See also J. P. Powell, E. Barrett, and V. Shanker, 'How Academics View Their Work', *Higher Education* 12 (3) 1983, pp. 297–313.

'overall body of knowledge in their subject' (compared to 94 per cent for journal articles. The monograph, for many researchers, remained a vital output not just in terms of developing knowledge in their field but in terms of the basis for career progression. One respondent in the survey was taken as typical, noting that the monograph 'remains the gold standard for career success (appointments; promotion) in my discipline.'[94] Libraries played an important part in the generation of these numbers, with many research offices working closely with librarians submitting texts to the REF and, indeed a library created at the REF offices to help distribute and account for materials.

The shifts in demands from the REF, notably a move towards open access, reflects a set of trends in scholarly communications. This self-reflexive analysis of how knowledge is created and disseminated has had more attention given to it over the last few years as a result of the disruption both posed and promised by digital innovation. The importance of funding bodies, whether governmental in the UK or philanthropic, such as the large US organisations, such as the Ford Foundation, also play a role in mapping research to desired outputs. Scholarly communication, of course, has a number of definitions. The Association of Research Libraries (ARL)' toolkit suggests 'the system through which research and other scholarly writings are created, evaluated for quality, disseminated to the scholarly community, and preserved for future use. The system includes both formal means of communication, such as publication in peer-reviewed journals, and informal channels, such as electronic listservs.'[95] Scholarly communications, as the University College London Library defined the process in 2010, can be seen as 'the method and route by which academic information is

[94] Cambridge and Oxford University Presses, 'Researchers' perspectives on the purpose and value of the monograph', Survey Results 2019, retrieved 6 November 2022 from global.oup.com/academic/pdf/perspectives-on-the-value-and-purpose-of-the-monograph.

[95] Association of Research Libraries, 'Scholarly Communication Toolkit: Scholarly Communication Overview', retrieved 6 November 2022 from acrl.libguides.com/scholcomm/toolkit.

passed from author to reader, via various intermediaries such as libraries and publishers'.[96] But it might also as Christine L. Borgman, states, be conceived as field of study: 'the study of how scholars in any field (e.g., physical, biology, social, and behavioural sciences, humanities, technology) use and disseminate information through formal and informal channels . . . [it] includes the growth of scholarly information, the relationships among research areas and disciplines, the information needs and uses of individual user groups, and the relationships among formal and informal methods of communication.'[97] In such a schema, libraries and monographs are linked by the use and dissemination of information, but are but one part of a much broader and more diverse research landscape, one that includes informal publications and personal contacts as well as journals or databases. Its study, one might argue, reflects the diversity of scholarly communications, and its change over time, while often analyses of scholarly communications, such as the one provided by ARL, are in many ways prescriptive. For example, the ARL toolkit suggests that libraries have opportunities to 'to advocate for and bring about positive change', and might, for example, 'strategically support open scholarship and positively respond to economic challenges of traditional scholarly publishing'. Interventions such as MIT Publishing's open access programme – organisationally part of the library structure – which includes 'Direct to Open' funding mechanism, in which libraries purchase back-run access but fund current open access publications, certainly point towards this as a possible future.[98]

[96] Quoted in Regazzi, *Scholarly Communications*, p. 48 (n.b., the original URL no longer exists can be accessed via web.archive.org/web/20100501201800/www.ucl.ac.uk/Library/scholarly-communication/index.shtml. See also D. N. Ocholla, 'Information-Seeking Behaviour by Academics: A Preliminary Study', *The International Information & Library Review* 28 (4) 1996, pp. 345–358.

[97] C. L. Borgman, 'Digital Libraries and the Continuum of Scholarly Communication', *Journal of Documentation*, 58 (4) 2000, pp. 412–430.

[98] See MIT Press, Direct to Open, retrieved 6 November 2022 from direct.mit.edu/books/pages/direct-to-open, libraries.mit.edu/scholarly/mit-open-access/ and libraries.mit.edu/scholarly/publishing/.

Librarians can also assist with the production of research through meta-analysis, particularly in the medical sciences, but also through assisting with literature searches. Despite notable exceptions, such as the number of citations for librarians at Bodleian Health Care Libraries, there is a risk that librarians are not asked to undertake such work, despite their expertise.[99] Members of the research team instead undertake such work.[100] Some of the work undertaken by librarians might be captures in the academic 'grass-roots' response to the REF, the 'Hidden REF' initiative.[101] Librarians, archivists and other GLAM (Galleries, Libraries, Archives, Museums) workers might be asked for suggestions for commercial digitisation projects. Indeed, many British collections are collaborations between libraries and commercial partners or, more recently, JISC-enabled projects, which have asked for librarians' input in the selection of materials.[102] As Aldus knew, publishing is as much about selling books as making books. By the nineteenth century, publishers had developed sophisticated systems for the selling and marking of books, including the development of warehouses, and agents who visited booksellers and other clients. Librarians today work closely with publishers, often meeting reps onsite or at conferences, and are clearly an important component in publishers' marketing plans. Paper catalogues are still sent regularly to acquisition teams, as well as specialist subject librarians, and are asked to comment on the usability of digital platforms and the types of materials that they would like to purchase.

Finally, at the end of the research cycle is the item of record. If the essence of a scientific experiment is its repeatability, the ability to check references is crucial to humanities research. Libraries offer the prospect of that. Libraries' collection development policies deal with this issue in

[99] 'Researchers', retrieved 6 November 2022 from nhs.bodleian.ox.ac.uk/help-and-training/researchers.

[100] H. K. Grossetta Nardini, J. Batten, M. C. Funaro, et al. 'Librarians as Methodological Peer Reviewers for Systematic Reviews: Results of an Online Survey' *Research Integrity and Peer Review* 4 (23) 2019.

[101] Hidden-ref.org.

[102] See the examples of Jisc library projects at beta. jisc.ac.uk/innovation/projects? topic=11.

different ways, with most library's stocks needing regular 'weeding', that is deaccessioning of materials no longer pertinent to the collection. An academic library is, for example, unlikely to retain a copy of every textbook. In the United Kingdom, the UK Research Reserve (UKRR) helps to share the burden of keeping a historic collection of every journal, with libraries deaccessioning their copies, if two others can be assured at other members of the UKRR. The next step will be a UK monograph research reserve. National libraries serve a purpose of national print archives, and this is also complemented by other initiatives, notably the Internet Archive's various projects, including the preservation of physical copies of books. Such archives are useful in terms of allowing access to information, but also in establishing priority of publication – that is, where do ideas first appear – and providing the item of record that can be checked. The 'citatation life' of a book may also be very long, particularly in the humanities, with items continuing to be cited or even finding their audience decades after publication.

4.2 Networks and Collaboration

In a such ways, libraries contribute to the book as a component within the process of scholarly communication. But it is of course a process. Looked at as an iterative loop, libraries also play roles at points along this chain of scholarly production, from the exploration of a research topic to its research, writing, review and then preservation. But scholarship is also an expansive process, one that is about connections, collaboration, and the development of what might still be termed a 'republic of letters'. While libraries are often thought of as a collection of individual texts, which are sort for a particular bit of information within them, they are actually powerful machines for making connections and amplifying the solitary thought or piece of data, giving it context, challenging it, and, crucially, placing a scholar within reach of the mind of another. Over the centuries, libraries have developed complicated ways of developing and enabling these networks, from catalogues to book exchanges.

Networks, we are increasingly told, have effects, some of which are unexpected.[103] The history of libraries is full of examples of connections between libraries that hint at the consequences of such interactions. For

---

[103] M. Kilduff and W. Tsai, *Social Networks and Organizations* (Sage, 2003).

example, inter-library loans, as we know call them, were familiar to the users of the great Library of Alexandria, helping to disseminate knowledge across the ancient world, while medieval 'catalogues', such as the early fourteenth century list of books held by the 183 Franciscan libraries in the British Isles suggest a certain amount of cooperation and perhaps exchange. Monastic libraries also facilitated exchange, and through these loans the development of personal relation between scholars and scribe.[104] The renaissance's republic of letters was in part underpinned by such loans; the desire to search out knowledge and the impulse among scholars to point out where it might be found informed Gabriel Naudé's 'fourth law of librarianship' which stated, 'that by this means (a catalogue) one may sometimes serve and please a friend when one cannot provide him with the work that he requires; by directing him to a place where he may find a copy as may be easily done with the assistance of these catalogues'.[105]

Networks were also facilitated by the central tools of librarianship: bibliographic records and common standards. In the middle of the nineteenth century, the great American librarian Charles Coffin Jewett proposed a general printed catalogue of libraries in the United States, in effect a national union catalogue, with standardised bibliographic records, using stereographic printing technology. In Jewett's scheme, individual libraries would be able to print annual additions to their collections, and the Smithsonian would print a general union catalogue of its own holdings, along with those held by public libraries. The idea would only come into fruition in 1952 with the United States' National Union Catalogue, although Jewett's plan influenced the German union catalogue which was begun in 1899.[106]

Nonetheless, the profession's joint efforts paved the way for a new era of cooperation. As the Swedish archivist and library historian Tomas Lidman notes, 'the standards and rules which had be devised for cataloguing

---

[104] N. Senocak, 'Early Fourteenth-Century Franciscan Library Catalogues: The Case of the Gubbio Catalogue (c. 1300)', *Scriptorium* 59 (1) 2005, pp. 29–50.

[105] Naudé, *Advice on Establishing a Library*, p. 12.

[106] 'Charles Jewett Proposes a National Union Catalogue, 1852', *Jeremy Norman's HistoryofInformation.com*, retrieved 6 November 2022 from historyofinformation .com/detail.php?id=2063.

materials during the latter half of the nineteenth century and which had been published in 1908 served as an impetus for libraries to cooperate with one another and coordinate their efforts'.[107] Modern libraries created networks in a host of ways, facilitated by a growing acceptance and definition of common standards and methods, and by exploring shared facilities, such as book storage. In England, the Central Library, based in London (and in 1973 incorporated into the newly established British Library) served as a centre for inter-library lending and coordination from 1916, with the assistance of the Carnegie United Kingdom Trust ('this is done by becoming the centre of a network of libraries'). Its librarian, Luxmoore Newcombe, worked over the next few decades to establish an effective national system. The Scottish Central Library in Edinburgh served a similar function. In 1921, the Trust again established the Scottish Central Library for Students, supplementing the resources of the fifteen Scottish county library service.[108] In 1929, the Trust also piloted a scheme for library cooperation based on union catalogues and inter-library lending based at the library of the Literary and Philosophical Society at Newcastle. This became a model for county libraries. Services such as the British Union Catalogue of Periodicals helped to support library services across the country. In the 1920s, the Association of University Teachers established the Joint Standing Committee on Library Cooperation. Such cooperation was also witnessed internationally, not least following the First World War and the creation of the League of Nations International Committee on Intellectual Cooperation. This body helped to develop such collaborative bibliographic projects as The Unusual Repertory of Printed Books, the International Library and the joint catalogue of Belgian libraries; the Committee was supplanted by UNESCO in 1945 (which 'inherited

---

[107] T. Lidman, *Libraries and Archives: A Comparative Study* (Chandos, 2012).

[108] 'The Service of Bibliographic Information in Great Britain and Ireland', in United Nations Archive, Geneva, R2200/5B/5027/404 – The International Co-ordination of Libraries – Correspondence with the International Institute of Intellectual Cooperation, retrieved 6 November 2022 from archives.ungeneva.org/the-international-co-ordination-of-libraries-correspondence-with-the-international-institute-of-intellectual-cooperation.

archives, library and quite some personnel from the League organisation'). And in 1927, the International Federation of Library Associations and Institutions (IFLA) was founded. Such activities had innumerable practical outcomes in terms of collection building and the research that was made possible. For example, international collaboration between librarians, academics and diplomats helped to establish the collections of the Institute of Historical Research, not just through the donations of printed materials, but in the gift of completed catalogue cards (in standard 125 mm × 75 mm format) from the Library of Congress (which had received a grant of $50,000 from John D. Rockefeller in 1927 for such bibliographic work).[109]

Collaboration and networking became buzzwords from the 1960s. Collaboration, via standards, helped to coordinate cataloguing across library systems, develop book storing and purchasing plans, and a host of professional development and library association activities. From the 1970s, it was clear that 'networking' was also going to be an important concept, particularly in relation to computers and automation. A series of conferences, colloquia and publications explored the ramifications for libraries of all kinds. Such were the implications of the information technology revolution that began in the 1970s represented a transformation, with the prospect of a 'radical departure from libraries as we have come to know them.' Technology of all kinds, as well as rising demands among a wider education population, stimulated the need for more widespread and sophisticated library provision: 'Carbon paper, typewriters, photocopy machines and microfilm are all products which radically expedite and change the possibilities for this type of library cooperation.'[110]

---

[109] United Nations Archive, Geneva, R2200/5B/5027/404 – The International Co-ordination of Libraries – Correspondence with the International Institute of Intellectual Cooperation, retrieved 6 November 2022 from archives.unge neva.org/the-international-co-ordination-of-libraries-correspondence-with-the-international-institute-of-intellectual-cooperation; C. A. Pernet, 'Twists, Turns and Dead Alleys: The League of Nations and Intellectual Cooperation in Times of War', *Journal of Modern European History* 12 (3) 2014, pp. 342–358.

[110] L. Brock, 'Why Networks for Libraries', *Law Library Journal* 70, 1977, pp. 55 & 58.

The contours of such collaboration became clearer over the 1980s, and was perhaps a change in extent, rather than radical revolution in type. The spread and adoption of the World Wide Web in the 1990s created more profound challenges, as libraries began to harness and then adapt to the web and its transformation of research practices. The ability to provide information online instantly, the growth of mass digitisation and academic publications shift to born digital publication has challenged the role of libraries as collaborators with publishers. While libraries still act as intermediaries (and invisible licensers and gatekeepers) between readers and content, it is an uneasy relationship, and one that is not readily apparent to many academics accessing materials. As Lidman notes, 'automatic bibliography generators could be integrated into existing systems and licensing a vast variety of electronic publications rendered many inter-library loans irrelevant. Integrative library systems were no longer within the sphere of interest of libraries alone. Commercial agents recognised new markets. As a result, national libraries shifted their focus and recognised the need to reach solutions not as separate institutions, but through cooperative endeavours.'[111] In response to such challenges, libraries have, as the final section shows, self-reflexively attempted to expand and develop their role within higher education, emphasising services and expertise as much as collections and space (while also dramatically reconfiguring those, too).

Library and cultural institutional collaborations such as Europeana and the Digital Public Library of America have shown the potential, as well some of the limits, of online aggregation of library material. Both these projects helped to create new online content, but primarily served as aggregators and coordinators of digitised materials created by other institutions. Such projects helped to focus government and philanthropic funding, such as the use of Horizon 2020 grants in the European Union, to develop the platform, standards and undertake discrete projects such as Europeana 1914–1918 and Europeana Newspapers. However, such sites sometimes lacked the technical infrastructure, resources and agility of commercial projects and, in particular that marketing resources to stake out a well-known space on the web or be promoted and used by research or public libraries. While there are clearly

---

[111] Lidman, *Libraries and Archives*.

challenges to the information landscape, as libraries move into the middle years of the twenty-first century, it is apparent that they remain an important part of a wider, international research network – and one that is not just limited to libraries. As Lindman notes, 'IFLA drafted a strategic plan in 2009 for the next five years. Among the explicit goals was improving access to information, which was a way of encouraging "the library and information sector to work with partners and users to maximise the potential of digital technology to deliver services that enable seamless and open access by users to cultural information resources"'.[112] In 2022, the Arts and Humanities Research Council published its strategic plan for the subsequent three years. Libraries are not heavily mentioned, but where they are, they are placed in the context of collaboration and research networks: digital scholarship fellowships at the Library of Congress, grants to the GLAM sector to demonstrate their 'significant role in building communities' and to 'directly link research and professional practice' through GLAM fellowships. At the same moment, the former head of Research England, David Sweeney, argued that the work of librarians (along with other research professionals such as technicians and research managers) should be included in any future assessment of research:

> Our research teams now include experts with a range of professional responsibilities, whether they be technicians, statisticians, librarians, research managers and so on. In considering research assessment the work of those teams should be assessed appropriately, not just the outputs which bear the names of the principal investigators and some colleagues. These discussions are less well developed in the theory and even further from a delivery mechanism.[113]

---

[112] Lidman, *Libraries and Archives*.

[113] UKRI, *Strategic Delivery Plan 2022–2025*, retrieved on 6 November 2022 from www.ukri.org/wp-content/uploads/2022/09/AHRC-010922-StrategicDeliveryPlan2022.pdf; L. Brassington, *Research Evaluation: Past, Present and Future* (Hepi, 2022), retrieved on 6 November 2022 from www.hepi.ac.uk/wp-content/uploads/2022/09/Research-Evaluation-Past-present-and-future.pdf.

But as these examples show, libraries have always been in the business of connecting books and other materials with people, and in the process collaborating with other libraries and the wider research world. Book formed the currency in an 'economy of knowledge'; like banks, libraries helped this intellectual capital to flow and grow.

4.3 Acknowledging Networks

The physical links between libraries and the academic book inform other, less tangible connections between the stacks and the scholars that use them. Less visible, perhaps, than buildings and codices, the processes and networks that these places and objects help to create and maintain are remarkably important to academia and the wider world. Academic books are clearly central to scholarly communications and the research process; libraries are similarly an important element of these processes, albeit arguably one less closely studied.[114]

Books can often speak of these intellectual entanglements more clearly. Think, for example, of the networks, academic hierarchies and scholarly obligations that are made visible, if only in part, in the 'paratextual' components of a book: the prefaces and acknowledgement pages of monographs. These oft-skipped sections of frequently formulaic prose help to service debts of gratitude as well allowing the author to situate themselves in relation to a school of thought and, perhaps, allow a certain amount of cultural or scholarly capital to adhere to their work. Here, as Blaise Cronin, one of the founders of what has been termed acknowledgement studies, reminds us, 'influence is operationalized as acknowledgement'.[115] While such litanies of appreciation are often formulaic and, as students of the burgeoning field of acknowledgement studies have noted, discipline-specific in terms of their formulation, length and degree of formality, help reveal the patterns of association, influence of mentorship, and other aspects

---

[114] There are moves within the sector to surface more of librarians', and other research professional's work in 'The Technician's Commitment'; see www.rluk .ac.uk/rluk-technician-commitment.

[115] B. Cronin, *The Scholar's Courtesy: The Role of Acknowledgement in the Primary Communication Process* (Taylor Graham, 1995), p. 1.

of authority and hierarchy within the academy (as well as offering on occasion intellectual terrain for rebellion, revenge and point-scoring; similar processes can be observed in the author-citing practices in the papers of the hard sciences).

As such, these paratextual components of a book constitute a modern form of the 'republic of letters', a contemporary echo of the scholarly communities that developed and sometimes thrived in early-modern Europe. The loan or sale of books, often across geographical boundaries, along with the sharing of ideas and intellectual materials that enabled them to be written, helped to embody and create these scholarly communities. And, as Anthony Grafton has elegantly demonstrated, the practicalities of book production in early-modern Europe were also central to the building and maintenance of such cultural connections. Intellectual and financial debts, the input of printers and their assistants, notably the men, women and, sometimes, children employed as correctors as the work moved from manuscript original to typesetting and, finally, to the printed work, all contributed not just to the physical creation of the book, but to networks of obligations, friendships and respect. Again, these networks and hierarchies are often visibly embodied in the paratextual elements of early modern books, notably the grand dedications to a monarch, nobleman or influential cleric, but also in the subscription pages of texts published in the eighteenth century or in the dedicatory verses or prefaces that accompany so many works, such as Ben Jonson's eulogy 'To the Reader' opposite William Shakespeare's portrait in the First Folio (1623) or Edmund Halley's preface (with his Latin poem) to Newton's *Principia* (1687) – to take two high spots of seventeenth-century printing.

Such expressions are important sources for the history of the book or for intellectual history. These expressions of thanks, listings of conferences and seminars, indigenous land right acknowledgements, and notes of appreciation for funders may also, in humanities books at least, be accompanied by acknowledgements of libraries or archives and expressions of thanks to librarians or archivists (who, it might be noted, are usually anonymous) – or even on occasion the settling of scores. Here, these paratextual elements offer a way of seeing the role libraries play in research (and the creation of academic books). Scholarly communications researchers have begun to explore how this might be done, as Joshua Finnell has outlined:

Academic libraries have been at the center of many of these endeavors, often pushing open access initiatives on their campuses, building digital repositories, hosting Zotero [reference management software] workshops for faculty and students, and assisting scholars in negotiating author rights for their work. Libraries are pivotal nodes in almost every intellectual network. However, even with the development of new metrics in paratextual evaluation, the work of libraries and librarians continues to be obscured. This is because the libraries lurk in the most overlooked paratextual element: the acknowledgement.[116]

Several studies have begun to provide a better understanding of this field. One, focussing on graduate theses, examined non-humanities subjects (civil engineering and geography, along with history) and noted that mentions appear throughout the text, albeit in methods or bibliography sections of dissertations and theses. As might be expected, acknowledgements are much more prevalent in history dissertations, appearing in around a quarter of these texts.[117] Another exploratory study by some of the same researchers, which examined a sample of science journal articles found a relatively low number of examples, often connected to natural history and institutions with important historical collections of artefacts but suggested that the methodology, with further improvements, could be a fruitful avenue of research.[118] The relatively

---

[116] J. Finnell, 'Much Obliged: Analyzing the Importance and Impact of Acknowledgements in Scholarly Communication', *Library Philosophy and Practice* (2014), retrieved on 6 November 2022 from http://eprints.rclis.org/25428/1/Finnell_Much%20Obliged.pdf.

[117] D. E. Hubbard, S. Laddusaw, J. Kitchens, and R. Kimball, 'Demonstrating Library Impact through Acknowledgment: An Examination of Acknowledgments in Theses and Dissertations', *The Journal of Academic Librarianship* 44 (3) 2018, pp. 404–411.

[118] D. E. Hubbard and S. Laddusaw, 'Acknowledgment of Libraries in the Journal Literature: An Exploratory Study', *Journal of Data and Information Science* 5 (3) 2020, pp. 178–186.

new field of acknowledgements research lacks an extensive research base, particularly in relation to libraries. Where research has taken place, a form of research that is by necessity time-consuming (even if part of the research makes used of digital, bibliometric methods), it focuses on the potential for that data to support the narratives that libraries tell about themselves to help shore up funding and also, as one study concluded, potentially to be used by US tenure-track librarians as further evidence in their promotion or tenure dossiers. Acknowledgement studies have proved to be a richer vein for linguistic analysis, drawing on these paratextual, and often relatively formulaic, texts to analysis different disciplinary uses of language. Such linguistic tropes were seen as an important differentiator in one study of an African university library acknowledgment practices. Acknowledgements have also proved to be a useful source for investigations into gender bias in supervision/student arrangements.[119] As important as such studies can be, they are not necessarily focussed on the qualitative exploration of the role library within the wider habits and practices of scholarly communications and the production of research, and there remains the possibility for useful future research here.

While we lack an extensive analysis of the potential data within acknowledgements, they do point to the relationship between libraries and the academic book, as well as highlighting some of the distinctive features of that relationship. There is clearly a more obvious link between most of the humanities and libraries that there is between libraries and the social and hard sciences. Humanities books, the evidence and anecdotal experience suggests, are more likely to highlight the studies use of collections held by libraries, and the assistance of librarians in locating materials. Libraries as a place to write or think might also be referenced, not least those that offer fellowships. Libraries'

---

[119] S. Bangani, D. Mashiyane, M. Moyo, and G. Makate, 'In/gratitude? Library Acknowledgement in Theses and Dissertations at a Distinguished African University', *Library Philosophy and Practice* 1 (2020), pp. 1–33. H. Meek, 'Thanks for All the Support'-An Evaluation Of Gender Bias In PhD Supervision', *CHERE@LU Working Paper Series* (Lancaster University) 1 (May 2019).

important stock of scientific literature and, vitally, management of subscriptions to often very expensive scientific journals, are less likely to be highlighted, despite the library's importance. It does suggest that the library as a physical place is something that scientists place less importance upon; for many, the laboratory offers a similar setting, both in terms of access to resources and social stimulation.

Finally, the hints of personal competition that can sometimes surface in acknowledgements are also a reminder that libraries – or librarians – don't always collaborate as the vision of the republic of letters might prefer them to. While librarians as a profession have a tendency towards collaboration, evidenced in the sharing of standards and the many professional and specialist library associations; but they also compete in terms of collections. Libraries, for example, like to boast the numbers of volumes that they hold, and rare book and special collections libraries have often competed for acquisitions or donations.

5 The New Normal?

5.1 A Hybrid World

In 2007, Jeff Gomez published *Print is Dead: Books in Our Digital*, arguing that the digital revolution witnessed in the music publishing industry (e.g., Napster and the Apple Music store) presented an inevitable agenda for change for publishers. He was not, of course, alone, with many 'web heads' predicting the end of print and the triumph of digital. Newspapers were clearly moving online, or were being replaced by digital media. Such prognosticators included some august voices. At the turn of the millennium, for example, the British Library predicted that most books would be digital within two decades. Gomez, as an industry insider, offered serious evidence that such views were likely to be right, and that publishers were planning for such a future – after all, the technologists were realising their plans: the Amazon Kindle e-reader launched in November 2007. For publishers, having seen the consequences of file-sharing on the music label profits, the ability to protect illicit copying or sharing of texts was a crucial concern, and the strong digital rights management embedded in the Kindle ecosystem (and the Barnes & Noble 'Nook') offered reassurance and a sweetener to publisher who were also concerned that Amazon would take too large a share of their profits.

Gomez, as far as we can tell fourteen years later, was perhaps only half right. The existence of this present Element as a physical object is one, small, testament to that. Yet, it is likely that the majority of its readers have accessed it online, either through its initial open access publication or later packaging as part of broader library-purchased access. It is possible that other readers have even purchased it themselves (if so, thank you). A not insignificant group, of course, may also be accessing it through the many illicit file-sharing sites, which have grown up in the shadows of Sci-Hub, which offers pirated access to the majority of online journals for free at point of use (albeit with legal ramifications for the user, along with – publishers are keen to claim – the possibility of malware, tracking and the implicit support for illegal online activities that potentially undermine the financial viability of the present scholarly communications business model). On a macro-level, digital publishing is in robust health, although as part of a broader publishing landscape, rather than one that replaced what went before it. Much like radio found a place alongside television following that medium's invention (and indeed, continued to have a wider reach in the UK in terms of absolute numbers) digital publications flourish alongside their print counterparts. In some areas, notably academic journals, the digital output is to all intents and purposes the primary output, with academic monographs and textbooks showing increasing signs of following this route (indeed, many library collection development policies, such as the Senate House Library, University of London, now explicitly state a preference for 'e-first'.[120] Trade publishing shows a preponderance towards print, although with digital (and Audible audiobooks) as an option. In response to the digital experience, there has also been a renaissance in book design, binding, and even in the quality of paper, with hardbacks in particular offering a visual statement that can be added to a room.

These are the observed outcomes, but behind the scenes, and concomitant transformation in the production of texts has taken place. Countering the view that 'print is dead', Gomez argued that publishers continue to animate the market and offers five reasons why they will 'still exist in a digital age.' Each of these reasons is detached from the physical product. Publishers still have a crucial role identifying, cultivating and compensating talent. These role in the value chain will, he argued, become more important as digital production expands dramatically, finding valuable 'signals' – as the phrase runs – in the 'noise' of YouTube or blogs. Gomez predates the explosion of social media, such as Twitter or TikTok, and the rise of open access scholarly communication.

The publisher's functions are likely to remain central to trade publishing, while the digital revolution has enabled many parts of the publishing process to be disintegrated. While functions such as indexing and copyediting were often outsourced, so increasingly are other functions such as marketing and editing. Publishing has witnessed a consolidation, with

---

[120] Senate House Library, University of London, Collection Development Policy, 27 June 2019, retrieved on 13 November 2022 from london.ac.uk/sites/default/files/shl/SHL%20Collection%20Management%20Policy%2031–7–19.pdf.

mergers and acquisitions such as that of Penguin and in 2013 and leading to the dominance of a handful of firms, known as the 'Big Five' Simon & Shuster, Penguin Random House, HarperCollins, Hachette Book Group, and Macmillan (at the time of writing a merger between Penguin Random House and Simon & Shuster is under review).

Academic publishing has successfully transitioned to a hybrid analogue/digital world, with digital processes now dominating production. Journals are produced through submission management systems, such as Clarivate's ScholarOne, and monographs brought into print or published online via Microsoft Word documents and annotated PDF files. Increasingly, many of the functions are outsourced, whether to individuals working on one component of production or to smaller firms that help to produce journals. The 'value-chain' of academic publishing is perhaps less obvious than that of trade publishing; or, at least the key aspects that Gomez and others identify, are less crucial. Gatekeeping is outsourced to academics themselves, as is peer and post-publication review.

Where then does the 'academic book' sit within this changing publishing landscape? The Big Five publishers all have interests in the education market, such as school or undergraduate textbooks, dictionaries and guides of various kinds, and some have strong academic imprints, such as Macmillan. Wiley or Oxford University Press are large academic presses, with less of a – although not negligible – focus on trade publishing. In 2019, the academic market is was estimated by Outsell to be \$28 billion. The total book market is around \$92 billion.[121] If these figures are any guide, the academic book represents more than a quarter of the total book market. For the foreseeable future at least, scholarship looks set to maintain its close

---

[121] '2021 STM Report: Global Research Trends and Transformation in Open Access Publishing, retrieved', *Enargo.com*, retrieved 13 November 2022 from www.enago.com/academy/2021-stm-report-global-research-trends/; 'Global Book Publishers Market Report (2021 to 2030) – COVID-19 Impact and Recovery – ResearchAndMarkets.com', *Business Wire.Com*, retrieved 13 November 2022 from www.businesswire.com/news/home/20210413005675/en/Global-Book-Publishers-Market-Report-2021-to-2030–COVID-19-Impact-and-Recovery–ResearchAndMarkets.com.

relationship with the monograph. Other forms of academic publishing, such as the scholarly edition or reference work, which are less reliant on serial reading, make heavy use of scholarly apparatus and sophisticated indexes and searching, look set to become primarily digital. Libraries, however, are likely to remain key intermediaries, purchasing or licencing commercial products, providing access for authorised faculty and students, and through their close connections to the world of digital scholarship, supporting open access and other non-commercial forms of reference work.

E-readers may also prove to be more important in the future, despite not reshaping the literary landscape as many expected.[122] Future-gazing in relation to digital readers is a fools' game – or at least the game of companies with large enough pockets to outspend rivals. While the Kindle was once thought to be enough of a threat to end physical books, much as the iPod saw off the CD, the physical book has had something of a renaissance (even more so than the remarkable return of vinyl recordings). The market for e-readers remains strong and viable, but largely leisure reading. In terms of demographics, it may even be focussed on an older generation, with younger people preferring, or simply accustomed, to screen reading, complemented by a revival in the printed book attested by the rise of 'BookTok' on the social network, TikTok. Conversations with current students and younger academics or postgraduates suggest a heterodox approach to scholarly reading, which reflects the range of ways that digital media are consumed today. Academic texts when consumed digitally are largely done so on laptops, phones or tablet (and sometimes converted into audio files for listening to, sometimes taking advantage of speeding up the playback).

If these trends will continue, digital/analogue hybrid consumption is likely to continue, paralleling the long-standing overlap of radio and television (although it is worth noting that digital consumption patterns are now challenging both these media). These patterns might also be disrupted by certain technologies, such as folding screens for phones, like

---

[122] A. Ballatore and S. Natale, 'E-readers and the Death of the Book: Or, New Media and the Myth of the Disappearing Medium', *New Media & Society* 18 (10) 2016, pp. 2379–2394.

as those developed by Samsung, or the reMarkable 2 tablet, which combines eInk technology with the ability to annotate with a digital pencil (and at the time of writing, Amazon just announced their Kindle Scribe, which combines reading with note taking).[123] Social media chatter among academics certainly suggests an interest in such a device. Finally, there remains a sense, particularly amongst humanists – as academics who spent long periods closely engaged with texts – that the digital experience of reading remains inferior to analogue. The potential affordances of the digital space, such as integration of audio-visual material, hyperlinking, community comments and so on do not seem to have shifted what is expected in terms of texts online. Digital books still attempt to copy their physical expression, while suffering still from some practical defects. Speed of scrolling, log-in and user verification remain points of friction, while notes remain problematic, and rarely function as well as a hypertext environment might. Scholarly questions of citation and edition also raise uncertainties in particular disciplines, as do matters of copyright (particularly in visual-heavy discipline such as art history, where online texts often lack the images in the printed copy due to rights restrictions and their associated costs). Such things, technologists might rightly assume, can be overcome with the development of better User Interfaces and User Experiences, the refinement of the legislative context, and the investment in better platforms and technologies by publishers over time. All these issues, even putting to one side the huge complexities of licencing and procurement, suggest a role for librarians as the intermediaries for such technologies.

5.2 Libraries Services

As Edward Maunde Thompson noted in 1889, it has been a very long time since librarians were just 'keepers of books'.[124] Libraries have long augmented their role as a storehouse of books with a host of activities that support their readers, and the phase 'library service' is a common way of description

---

[123] @martin_eve, 10:18am, 25 September 2022, *twitter.com*, retrieved 13 November 2022 from web.archive.org/save/https://twitter.com/martin_eve/status/157396509 5100727297.

[124] Quoted in Minter, 'Academic Library Reform', p. 34.

a library organisation, and is typically used in the United Kingdom to describe county or other regional libraries. Many library workers have their role described in terms of running or manage services. The term may also provide a description of the power relationships: libraries are in the service of their patrons, whether the general public, students or academics, depending on the type of library. Libraries assist in providing access to knowledge and the wider work of the organisations, professions or other groups that they support. Indeed, the situation that such a hierarchy describes has also attracted a range of critiques, such as suggesting collaboration is a better mode of operation that 'service', the personal cost of service, particularly when seen through the lens of gender or race.[125] The closure of buildings to readers during the Covid-19 pandemic also brought the concept of the 'library as a service' to the fore, stressing the numerous things that a library does – answering enquiries, advising on copyright, scanning and copying, assisting with institutional digital repositories, providing access to online materials, offering kerb-side or other 'click and collect' physical services – as opposed to 'just' being a building.[126]

This discourse drew on a growing trend to focus on the 'library as a service' from the end of the 1990s, when the library leaders and others began to grapple in earnest with what a library would look like in a digital age. The 'future of the library' or the 'library of the 21st century' was the subject of numerous reports, workshops and plenary lectures, suggesting a mix of confidence and unease at the potential change ahead; arguably, a quarter of the way through the twentieth-first century, the picture is still somewhat unclear.[127] However, two aspects have been

[125] L. Sloniowski, 'Affective Labor, Resistance, and the Academic Librarian', *Library Trends* 64 (4) 2016, pp. 645–666; V. Arellano Douglas and J. Gadsby, *Deconstructing Service in Libraries: Intersections of Identities and Expectations* (Litwin Books, 2020).

[126] For example, the thread at web.archive.org/web/20220926135944/https://twitter.com/brawbukes/status/1347482374037241856?s=20&t=w39ThzElOjpO0xzfdjJjFw.

[127] C. Closet-Crane, '(Re)Creating the Academic Library as Place for the 21st Century? A Critical Analysis of Discourse in Discussions of Academic Library

repeatedly highlighted: the library as a space, and the library as a service. These analyses move the concept of service on from earlier definitions, placing more of a focus on the potential for collaboration and creation of content – and possibly inflected by the notion of 'software as a service', which refers to cloud applications that can be expanded or shrunk to fit the organisation's needs. This vision of an academic library places less of a focus on the content of the library, but on the skills of the library staff, who are potentially collaborators with academics, offering training in information skills, advice on search strategies, copyright and intellectual property, research data management, open access, and helping with practical applications, such as the use of video suites, GIS toolkits, 3D printing spaces or business incubation.[128] Library staffing functions might also be focussed on such collaboration, with academic liaison and engagement officers providing a link between academic departments and the library's services. Librarians are also regularly cited as co-authors in literature reviews, notably among librarians working in medical libraries, and play important roles in academic/library subject or areas associations, such as SALALM – the Seminar on the acquisition of Latin American Library Materials.[129] Unique collections, including data and special collections,

Planning and Design', *ProQuest Dissertations and Theses*, Ph.D., Emporia State University, 2009, retrieved 13 November 2022 from www.proquest.com/doc view/205435199/abstract/424781C485384A4CPQ/1.

[128] For example, see the *Chronicle of Higher Education* 'Library of the Future' discussion (2022) and associated report at www.chronicle.com/events/vir tual/the-future-of-academic-libraries; many issues are also touched on in the Research Library Group Digital Shift Manifesto, retrieved 13 November 2022 from www.rluk.ac.uk/digital-shift/ and OCLC *New Model Library: Pandemic Effects and Library Directions* (2022), retrieved 13 November 2022 from www .oclc.org/content/dam/research/publications/2021/oclcresearch-new-model-library-a4.pdf.

[129] R. L. Hart, 'Collaborative Publication by University Librarians: An Exploratory Study', *The Journal of Academic Librarianship* 26 (2) 2000, pp. 94–99; M. L. Rethlefsen, A. M. Farrell, L. C. Osterhaus Trzasko, and T. J. Brigham, 'Librarian Co-authors Correlated with Higher Quality Reported Search Strategies in General Internal Medicine Systematic Reviews', *Journal of*

combined with digital scholarship expertise, digitisation studios and digital libraries and repositories also offer, and have been used, for significant research projects as well as innovative teaching programmes. Numerous examples abound: the Unlocking Mary Hamilton Papers project at the John Rylands Library (University of Manchester) had its public launch as this Element came to press.[130] Library space is also increasingly seen as a 'service', something that the closure of buildings during the pandemic brought into focus. As a post-Covid-19 OCLC report notes, 'building closures highlighted the importance of treating library spaces as a service that supports people coming together to use the library for different purposes.'[131] Clearly, libraries are set for ongoing change and development.

Within all these shifts, however, we can still see a role for books. A recent analysis of open shelves, for example, envisioned a hybrid environment, but one that still stressed the importance of the library as a space to consume academic books.[132] Libraries are experimenting with the placing of books, for example on wellbeing or the increasingly literature offering advice on post-graduate and academic careers, offering advice on publication, teaching methods, and the benefits of 'slow academia'. Providing speedy access to academic books, whether in print or online, and enabling serendipitous discovery and different modes of study remain vital activities for libraries. And there are also examples of libraries not just acquiring books, but collaborating on their – and similar academic outputs' – production. The Programming Historian, for example, an international, volunteer-driven project of ever-growing suite of online guides to digital history is partly

Clinical Epidemiology 68 (6) 2015, pp. 617–626; 'Seminar on the Acquisition of Latin American Library Materials', *American Library Association Affiliates*, retrieved on 13 November 2022 from www.ala.org/aboutala/affiliates/affiliates/salalm.

[130] *Unlocking the Mary Hamilton Papers*, www.maryhamiltonpapers.alc.manchester.ac.uk.

[131] L. Silipigni Connaway, Ixchel M. Faniel, and Brittany Brannon, *New Model Library: Pandemic Effects and Library Directions* (OCLC Research, 2021).

[132] 'Predicting the Role of Library Bookshelves in 2025 | Elsevier Enhanced Reader', retrieved 25 September 2022 from https://doi.org/10.1016/j.acalib.2017.06.019.

funded by the financial contribution of institutional partners, including libraries.[133] Similar support for platforms such as the Open Library of the Humanities, which allow the publication of open access journals, point to a possible future for open access monographs.[134] Yet, libraries have not generally been a base for monographic production, a potential innovation that was often mooted in the early twenty-first century, and which instead reside in University Presses or departments of scholarly communication or scholarship (or occasionally academic departments). Some notable presses reside within the library's organisational structure, such as at Stanford, MIT, Michigan or Temple.[135] The financial firepower of libraries has been bound up with the management of APC and 'Big Deals', a shorthand for large packages of journals which include open access publishing fees for the institution's faculty and postgraduates, which tend – at the moment – to exclude monographs. The picture is likely to change, not least in the UK as research funders move towards broader requirements for open access provision for books as well as journals from 2024.[136]

While libraries have not in become publishers (with the exception of some national libraries and some other specialised institutions or a few large university libraries, such as the Bodleian Library Publishing), many libraries are responsible for institutional digital repositories (using software such as DSpace), which contain many thousands of book titles in preprint form, many of which are available outside of the institution. This looks only set to grow as the demands for open access publishing increases. It is here, and as a key point of contact between academia and publishers that libraries and the academic book will continue to play an important role at least

---

[133] 'Our Supporters', *Programming Historian*, retrieved 13 November 2022 from programminghistorian.org/en/supporters.

[134] 'Monographs and Open Access', Brunel University London Library, retrieved on 13 November 2022 from www.brunel.ac.uk/life/library/ORR/Monographs-and-open-access.

[135] Greco, *Scholarly Publishing*, p. 157.

[136] www.ukri.org/what-we-do/supporting-healthy-research-and-innovation-cul ture/open-research/open-access-policies-review/implementing-our-open-access-policy.

through the middle of the twenty-first century, and possibly beyond. The academic book looks set to be a key field in the developing relationship between publishers, libraries and academic books. The transition from print to digital has largely been completed for journals, with certain disciplinary differences, such as art history's ongoing need for printed copies that include reproductions, and certain disciplines' use of moderated eprints (rather than peer review), notably mathematics, computer science, physics and economics use of ArXiv.org.

5.3 Libraries and the Future

Librarians might do well to have a couple of Naudé's recommended jasper stones to hand, needing their luck and guidance, and perhaps the globes he also recommended to try and map a route to the future. Taking a leaf from his text, it means continuing what works from the past, given that many library practices have been worn smoother over time until they offer as frictionless operation as possible, while embracing useful reform and technological change where it brings benefits. Naudé remained focused on who might use the library, and this surely remains true. As for the book, the monograph and its importance to academic seems certain (as certain as academia itself, in any case).[137] Some might conclude that there is too much at stake for publishers and academics as well as libraries (while they remain in control of budgets do, of course, have the ability to shape scholarly publishing's terrain) to change things dramatically.

Publishers may seek to remove the library almost totally, of course. It is not impossible to imagine publishers or aggregators of content selling directly to the student or the academic, in a kind of Netflix for textbooks or scholarly monograph (indeed some adverts from current online text-book sellers suggest that it is being proposed at the moment); academics are already accustomed to purchasing (i.e., licenced for their personal use) e-books of many trade or academic texts if pitched at the right price, and are often puzzled why libraries can't simply buy an e-book in the same way. Publishers have already begun to expand selling directly to readers,

---

[137] Naudé, *Advice on Establishing a Library*.

constituting 26 per cent of sales in 2019.[138] The licencing costs for e-books, which places many packages out of reach for many libraries, even those with deep pockets, surely incentivises those academics or students who can afford it to at least think about using such a service or buying e-books

But who really knows? Things change very slowly and then very fast; the transition from the print to the digital monograph may happen as profoundly as it did for the journal. Covid-19 is a reminder of how change can happen. The library as space and a service – and the home of the special collection – rather than a collection of current physical texts may be a safer bet in the long term. Ambitious trainee librarians might be well advised to pay attention to classes on licencing and procurement.

5.4 Artificial Intelligence and Data

Without wishing to sound like a TED talk or even the library equivalent of a 'tech bro', I have to admit, with some reluctance, that any consideration of the library and the academic book does have to give serious consideration to some of the buzz words of the moment. There are of course more valuable markets, and this may cause these various bubbles to pop or strike oil in other aspects of modern life, but given the importance of data and information to libraries, it seems prudent to give them some attention.

The consolidation in library management systems and in publishing point to large potential changes in the future. Discovery layers – what we once simply called the catalogue – might link ever more closely into publisher's platforms. Despite regulation about personal data, information about users might be aggregated in new ways, linked to classroom performance and attendance, or perhaps grant capture. The UK's departure from the EU has already raised questions about the longevity of the GDPR and has changed how libraries approach orphan works, making them more cautious in at least one case (the British Library's Spare Rib project, which had to take down an online archive that included materials digitised using an Orphan Works exemption).[139]

---

[138] Greco, *Scholarly Publishing*, p. 100.

[139] 'Spare Rib archive – possible suspension of access UPDATE', *Social Science Blog*, retrieved on 13 November 2022 from blogs.bl.uk/socialscience/2019/10/ spare-rib-update.html.

Such data might lead to insights about what works are popular and what might be published in the future, as well as a host of other potential decisions.

Machine learning and artificial intelligence (AI) continue to make astonishing leaps, while still provoking great uncertainty about their final trajectory, efficacy, copyright issues and inbuilt biases and privacy concerns, as well as more existential concerns.[140] Nonetheless, translation of texts into different languages, mass reading of papers or books for a host of patterns, artefacts or sematic objects are now possible, highly effective and affordable. It is not impossible to imagine asking an AI-informed search engine a question and it summarising its findings from a host of texts, perhaps found across Google Books (or a scholarly publisher's vast collection of specialised texts) and ranked in usefulness according to data derived from advanced library management systems and its user's linked social data (or citation indexes); indeed, between the submission of the draft of this Element and its printing, Microsoft's Copilot and Google's Gemini are racing to implement effective versions of such a search. Large Language Models (LLM) don not just summarise, but expand upon vast datasets of books (many derived from the scanning of academic libraries), creating the illusion – or even the reality – of a student essay or academic paper. Already, LLMs such as OpenAI's ChatGPT producing convincing poems, short stories, and student essays, amongst a host of other outputs. Truly logical, creative and critical thinking (Artificial General Intelligence) rather than the ability to extrude pre-existing thought into recognised patterns that give the impression of thinking may, of course, ultimately elude such tools, but such is the power and potential of existing LLMs, it may be hard to avoid being made unscrupulous use of them. To counter this, some might even suggest that many educational experiences (and even some academic interventions) are not so very different from the experience of some of these AIs, and many aspects may even be improved.

---

[140] This field is vert fast moving. For an insightful summary of the state-of-play, and reflections on the future, at the time of writing, see L. Demsey, 'Generative AI and libraries: 7 contexts', LorcanDemsey.net, retrieved 15 November 2023 from www.lorcandempsey.net/generative-ai-and-libraries-7-contexts.

Similar tools might serve as form of peer review, editorial assessment, or library purchasing analysis tools, either in collaboration with human academics, or left to its own devices. Already, librarians are experimenting and even deploying tools such as Claude AI, Gemini or ChatGPT to assist in cataloguing of current acquisitions.[141] Blockchain technologies might be deployed as a decentralised way to provide authoritative records of editions, texts and archives: a pilot at The National Archives is already exploring this potential.[142] In these potential futures, the book – or at least its contents – feeds directly into wider set of systems.

Less speculatively, there are other signs of important and often-fascinating developments in the relationship between libraries and what we call the academic book. It would be foolish to ignore demographic changes, as well as the challenges in academia and other professional fields. Library workers are more heterogenous than ever before, despite substantial barriers to equal gender, race and class access still being in place. This is reflected in attitudes and interests. The expansion of graduate education without a concomitant growth in academic jobs, indeed a vast contraction in many areas, has brought many early career or postgraduates into library work. The focus on the library as a collaborative space has encouraged some library leaders, such as Dame Lynne Brindley, former head of the British Library, to focus on the specialised, subject-based skills of librarians over the requirement for traditional, formal library school qualifications.[143] Some of these librarians are likely to make their own contribution to the academic book, with their own texts, as well as collaborating with academic colleagues on future projects in ways that will undoubtedly shape the new library; many are engaged in what is known as the 'critical librarianship'

---

[141] See for example R. Brzustowicz, 'From ChatGPT to CatGPT: The Implications of Artificial Intelligence on Library Cataloging', *Information Technology and Libraries* 42 (3) 2023.

[142] A. Green, 'Trustworthy Technology: The Future of Digital Archives', The National Archives, 5 June 2018, retrieved 12 November 2023 from blog.nationalarchives.gov.uk/trustworthy-technology-future-digital-archives.

[143] L. Brindley, 'The Future Roles of Research Libraries', NLB Singapore, retrieved on 13 November 2022 from www.youtube.com/watch?v=gfSbzhxp9uI.

movement.[144] Some sense of this can be found in the numerous decolonisation projects which libraries are intimately involved in. For example, the Bodleian Library received a $250,000 grant from the Mellon Foundation for a project 'We Are our History', looking at issues of race and decolonisation in the collections, audience and staffing.[145] Indeed, libraries can claim to be central in supporting efforts towards the decolonisation processes in Higher Education.[146] Libraries have acted across the globe to look to build collections more inclusively. The representation of the academic book within library collections is now likely to include voices from the global south or indigenous scholars and approaches to knowledge. Projects to revise cataloguing standards, updating outdated or exclusionary categories, as well as providing proper provenance records for historical materials, will also help to surface these strands in the collections, helping to ensure that the academic book truly reflects global knowledge.[147] The academic book and the library, it is to be hoped, have a much more expansive future ahead.

[144] R. Delgado and J. Stefancic, 'Why Do We Tell the Same Stories?: Law Reform, Critical Librarianship, and the Triple Helix Dilemma,' *Stanford Law Review* 42 1989, pp. 207–225; J. Barr-Walker and C. Sharifi, 'Critical Librarianship in Health Sciences Libraries: An Introduction', *Journal of the Medical Library Association: JMLA* 107 (2) 2019, pp. 258–264; E. Drabinski, 'What Is Critical about Critical Librarianship?', *Art Libraries Journal* 44 (2) 2019, pp. 49–57.

[145] For an example of the wider Higher Education context, see 'Cambridge Responds to Legacies of Slavery Enquiry', University of Cambridge, retrieved 22 November 2022 from www.cam.ac.uk/stories/legacies-of-enslavement-inquiry.

[146] C. Kamposiori, 'Developing Inclusive Collections: Understanding Current Practices and Needs of RLUK Research Libraries', RLUK report, 13 July 2023, retrieved 12 November 2023 from zenodo.org/records/8143097.

[147] Cataloging Lab, retrieved 22 September 2022 from cataloginglab.org.

Cambridge Elements $\equiv$

Publishing and Book Culture

SERIES EDITOR
Samantha Rayner
University College London

Samantha Rayner is Professor of Publishing and Book Cultures at UCL. She is also Director of UCL's Centre for Publishing, co-Director of the Bloomsbury CHAPTER (Communication History, Authorship, Publishing, Textual Editing and Reading) and co-Chair of the Bookselling Research Network.

ASSOCIATE EDITOR
Leah Tether
University of Bristol

Leah Tether is Professor of Medieval Literature and Publishing at the University of Bristol. With an academic background in medieval French and English literature and a professional background in trade publishing, Leah has combined her expertise and developed an international research profile in book and publishing history from manuscript to digital.

ABOUT THE SERIES

This series aims to fill the demand for easily accessible, quality texts available for teaching and research in the diverse and dynamic fields of Publishing and Book Culture. Rigorously researched and peer-reviewed Elements will be published under themes, or 'Gatherings'. These Elements should be the first check point for researchers or students working on that area of publishing and book trade history and practice: we hope that, situated so logically at Cambridge University Press, where academic publishing in the UK began, it will develop to create an unrivalled space where these histories and practices can be investigated and preserved.

Cambridge Elements ≡

Publishing and Book Culture

Academic Publishing

Gathering Editor: Jane Winters

Jane Winters is Professor of Digital Humanities at the School of Advanced Study, University of London. She is co-convenor of the Royal Historical Society's open-access monographs series, New Historical Perspectives, and a member of the International Editorial Board of Internet Histories and the Academic Advisory Board of the Open Library of Humanities.

ELEMENTS IN THE GATHERING

The General Reader and the Academy: Medieval French Literature and Penguin Classics
Leah Tether

The Edited Collection: Pasts, Present and Futures
Peter Webster

Old Books and Digital Publishing: Eighteenth-Century Collections Online
Stephen H. Gregg

Reading Peer Review: PLOS ONE and Institutional Change in Academia
Martin Paul Eve, Cameron Neylon, Daniel Paul O'Donnell, Samuel Moore, Robert Gadie, Victoria Odeniyi and Shahina Parvin

Publishing Scholarly Editions: Archives, Computing, and Experience
Christopher Ohge

Printed in the United States
by Baker & Taylor Publisher Services